HIGH SCHOOL DANCE

stories

STARBUCK O'DWYER

HIGH SCHOOL DANCE

STARBUCK O'DWYER

GCP
GREEN CHAIR PUBLISHING   NEW YORK

ISBN 13: 978-0972162470

Copyright © 2016 by Starbuck O'Dwyer

All rights reserved under International and Pan-American Copyright Conventions. No part of this book may be reproduced or transmitted in any form or by any means, electronic or mechanical, including but not limited to photocopying, electronic mail, recording or by any information storage or retrieval system, without permission in writing from the copyright holder. Names and characters (other than the author's immediate family) are the product of the author's imagination or are used fictitiously, and any resemblance to any actual persons, living or dead, events or locales is entirely coincidental. Trademarks and service names have been used throughout this book and are owned by their respective trademark holders. Rather than insert a trademark notation at each occurrence of the name, the publisher states that all such trademarks are used in an editorial manner without any intent to infringe upon the trademark.

Also by Starbuck O'Dwyer

RED MEAT CURES CANCER

GOLIATH GETS UP

HOW TO RAISE A GOOD KID

About the Author

Starbuck O'Dwyer, a native of Rochester, New York and a graduate of Princeton, Oxford and Cornell, writes novels, essays, short stories, screenplays and music under his given middle name. His critically-acclaimed novel, *Red Meat Cures Cancer* (Random House/Vintage Books), won two national writing awards for humor, appeared on several best-seller lists, and was a featured selection of the 2007 One Book One Vancouver reading program. His writing, which has been described as "comic genius" by *Kirkus Reviews*, has been published in forums as diverse as *Entertainment Weekly*, *Flaunt*, *Toro*, *Japanophile*, *the Journal News*, *PW Daily* and the *Boston Globe*, and he has appeared on over 350 radio and television programs including guest spots on ESPN, WGN, Fox, NBC and Voice of America. His memoir, *How to Raise a Good Kid*, was a finalist in both the 2012 Indie Reader Discovery Awards (parenting) and the 2011 ForeWord Reviews Book of the Year Awards (essay and humor categories) and has been translated into Chinese. Similarly, his novel, *Goliath Gets Up*, was a finalist in the 2012 Indie Reader Discovery Awards (humor) and has also been translated into Chinese. In addition, songs that O'Dwyer composed have been licensed by both the Telemundo and Country Music Television networks and featured in several of their shows.

For my family and friends,
especially my wife, Kris, and my sister, Pam

Table of Contents

Preface 1

1 The Wall 3

2 Bringing Home the Iron 15

3 Rock and Roll 28

4 Heroes 35

5 Failure 44

6 Competition 54

7 Heartbreak 65

8 Fame 72

9 Prom 81

10 Trust 89

11 Friendship 98

12 Sprink Break 109

How To Raise A Good Kid Sample Chapters 122

PREFACE

Welcome to *High School Dance*. I'm glad you're here. This book is the culmination of a project that began in 2008, shortly after my wife and I welcomed our son to the world. Like most first-time fathers, I felt a new and profound sense of responsibility and immediately became determined to pass along every lesson I believed was important. So even though my pride and joy was only drooling, pooping and sleeping at this point, and was years away from absorbing his dad's hard-earned wisdom, I refused to let any of those pesky details get in my way.

First, I made a list of the events of my childhood that taught me the most, the ones that made the biggest impressions, both good and bad. This exercise forced me to revisit many harrowing experiences such as batting zero in little league baseball, my chronic addiction to a blanket, my disastrously unsuccessful try-out for the role of Winthrop in *The Music Man*, and the time I mooned the entire sixth grade. I wanted to let my son know whatever hardship he might face; his father had already been there, learned something of value and survived. I also wanted to let him know about all the fun and joy I experienced as a child and the love my parents showed me.

After compiling my list, however, I realized it wasn't going to be enough. What if, God forbid, I wasn't around to tell him the full story behind each enumerated item? I couldn't bear the thought so I decided to turn the list into a book of stories about my childhood. Over time, the project evolved into two books: one about my grade school years, *How to Raise a Good Kid*, and one about my junior and senior high school years, *High School Dance*.

I truly hope you enjoy these collections. Few times in life are more memorable than our school years. Humiliation, heartbreak and failure are abundant, and that's on a good day. No matter who you are, coming of age is exciting, confusing and sometimes downright dangerous, and I've tried to capture both the agony and the ecstasy. My wife and I were fortunate enough to add a daughter to our family in the intervening years and my great hope is that she and her brother will someday read these stories, learn a few lessons, come to know their father even better, and remember, above all, how much I love them.

1
THE WALL

By the end of sixth grade, I had it all: a plastic case filled with official NFL pencils, a desk to put it in, and a purpose as one of the school safeties. I had taco Tuesday, pizza Friday and chocolate milk cost eight cents. I had friends, Field Day and free reign to check out any book I wanted from the library. I could even go to the bathroom without a teacher's aide. Yes, I was flying higher than the tater tots I liked to launch from my cafeteria spoon. I knew the teachers, the principal, and my place at Thornell Road Elementary, and scoring points on this perfectly-balanced pinball machine was so easy I believed nothing would change when I moved on to junior high school. Little did I know the new machine would tilt early and often.

I wore white on the first day of seventh grade, a carefully coordinated selection of bone-colored corduroy pants and a soft, creamy velour shirt with a collar. I was still innocent. I didn't swear. I didn't talk back to adults. I respected authority. And though I'd heard of the book *Oh God, It's Me, Margaret*, I hadn't read it and had no idea what it was about. I had never watched cable TV, been online, broken a bone or suffered the loss of a loved one. I had two loving parents, a warm home and little knowledge of violence, poverty or strife. In my eyes everything was possible and as I stepped from my father's car to the curb of Barker Road Junior High School, I expected this life of hand-written notes in my lunch bag and smiley faces on my homework to continue along the same trajectory.

It was a sumptuous September day, still full of the warmth of summer but ripe with the promise of fall and the smell of new sneakers. Peering around, all I saw were strange ninth graders, stranger eight graders, and wholly unidentifiable seventh graders from elementary schools other than mine. Everybody seemed so much taller than me but I refused to let their size or my failure to recognize them throw me. I was in the big show now and I needed to act like I belonged.

Inside, the halls offered nothing but a blur of backpacks and bodies. Clinging to a copy of my new schedule, I tried to find my homeroom but the orderliness of a simple elementary coatroom had been replaced by the chaos of lockers, bells and a crowded, unfamiliar maze. Barker Road was only one mile from my previous school, but it felt like Neptune. I arrived at Room 224 and found a desk toward the back, hoping I'd see a face from my Thornell Road days. The novelty of the situation was energizing but the only faces I saw were ones plagued with insecurity, a disease of sorts that would drive many to act in ways they never would have considered only months before.

My first class was music where I met Mr. Whitney, a teacher still clinging to the 1960s on the cusp of 1980. He had the requisite long hair tied back in a ponytail, bell-bottom jeans, a denim vest he wore over various concert t-shirts and a fervent belief all music since the Beatles was derivative with one exception: Gentle Giant. I'd never heard of Gentle Giant but I was ready to believe him and accept his peculiarities without judgment. Some of my classmates, however, were not and in between Mr. Whitney's earnest soliloquys about the genius of John Lennon and his attempt to teach us *Let It Be* on the recorder, I heard kids mocking him. They made fun of his hair, his clothes, his breath (which allegedly was bad) and his name, labeling him Prick Twitney, Dick Witless and an assortment of other awful monikers. I was accustomed to respecting my teachers so I was confused and conflicted by this behavior and increasingly uncomfortable. This was a level of cynicism and sarcasm I'd never seen before.

There were other strange things happening at Barker Road that made the cinder block hallways feel like a frightening funhouse. One of my closest friends, who I'd spent countless hours with in fifth and sixth grade, became dissatisfied with his social stature overnight and determined rising above it meant jettisoning me. Obsessively, he curried favor with kids he saw emerging as the most popular from the amalgam of new seventh graders. He stopped including me in trips to the mall, sleepovers and Sharky's, a roller-skating rink we loved. Suddenly, he was always busy and when I caught wind of a planned gathering and asked if I could come, he made up ridiculous excuses like the car was too full or his parents didn't want more than a certain number of kids attending, cruelly lying and causing me a new kind of pain. This was my introduction to exclusion and sadly, due to my guilelessness, it took me a month or so to catch on. I was Navin Johnson from *The Jerk*, a complete idiot who looks at incoming gunfire and bullet ridden cans all around him and thinks the assailant is shooting at the cans. I suffered through many humiliating conversations before I gave up on our friendship and quietly let go.

This same so-called friend (I'd say frenemy but the word hadn't been invented yet so let's call him Dick) wasn't done with me. Competition for female attention had gone from an intramural level in sixth grade to a Division 1 varsity sport in seventh, and Dick played to win. There was one girl in particular every boy in the school had fallen in love with at first sight. Michelle was as friendly as she was cute and when she walked into my home economics class wearing a blue gingham shirt, blue jeans, clogs and perfectly feathered hair, I was monumentally smitten. Of course, so was Dick and whenever he saw me speaking to Michelle, he would come up behind me and push my books from the crook of my arm or try to trip me or shout in my ear - anything to make me look bad. Then he'd laugh a forced laugh like we were sharing the joke together. I looked so foolish I figured it killed any chance I had of every getting close to Michelle so I said goodbye to her and hello to unrequited love.

A month into school, the happiness I'd felt in sixth grade was gone and my prized NFL pencil case had been stolen. Every time I entered school, I felt a mix of fear, insecurity, heartsickness and dread. Excluded by old friends, disparaged by older kids and pining for Michelle, I hated going to Barker Road and felt a desperate longing to belong to *something* or *someone*, all of which explained my willingness to join a group of strangers. It was a Friday at dismissal when I saw some boys walk past their buses and begin heading toward the village of Pittsford. Two miles away, the village sat astride the Erie Canal with shops, restaurants, churches and the public library. I guessed the group was going to get food and followed behind them, contemplating how to introduce myself.

"Hey, can I join you guys?" I shouted half out of breath, running to catch up.

Nobody said anything, so in the absence of a negative I assumed a positive. Walking past homes and people, I forgot for a moment I didn't know these boys and acted as if I was a full-fledged member of the group, imagining us a troupe of explorers forging our way to the village the way Vasco de Gama forged his way to India. As we got closer to the village, we began pizza places I hoped they'd enter.

"You guys getting pizza?" I asked, like an *Animal House* reject.

There was no reply but no one hit me either so I continued to follow the group of seven as they approached and then walked beneath the main bridge over the canal to a wooded pathway that ran along the water.

"Where are you guys headed?" I asked nervously.

"Scum-jumping," the biggest boy said without looking back.

Feeling like a rube, I didn't dare ask what that meant. Half a mile down the canal, we came to a clearing and a second bridge covered with rust except for the stainless steel train tracks running through its center. Without hesitation, the gang I'd attached myself to walked on to the bridge and began shedding clothes. In seconds, they were in their underwear and I was in a very awkward position.

"Are you jumping or not?" the leader asked.

"In there?" I said, pointing to the canal which lay 35 feet below the bridge.

"Duh!"

"Sure, sure," I said, facing the full weight of peer pressure and commencing to drop my pants. "Are you sure it's safe? We're awfully high up,"

"Oh, grow a pair, will ya?"

"Just looks a little far down, that's all," I said, surveying the muddy water from our perch.

Moments later, my protest having fallen on deaf ears, I stood in my skivvies on the ledge of a bridge with a group of kids I didn't know about to jump to my likely death.

"I heard there's a dead cow floating in there," the red-headed kid standing next to me said. "Make sure you don't hit it when you go in."

"But I can't see anything beneath the water. It's too dark," I said in a panic.

"You just have to hope," he said. "Some say it's only a severed head."

"That's encouraging," I replied.

One by one, the boys jumped. Hoots, hollers, thumps and splashes followed as each hit the water and resurfaced alive and exuberant much to my surprise. Soon I was alone on the bridge.

"Jump!" they shouted. "Jump!"

How did I get here? I thought as I stared down at the scummy depths of the Erie Canal in my underwear praying I wouldn't hit the dead cow head. If I was going to fit in, I knew I had to jump but I was terrified and felt so far away from anyone who knew or cared about me. Something told me I would find myself in these situations more and more as I got older and I didn't like it. Did I want to fit in this badly? The kids exiting the water looked alright so maybe I would be okay but who knew? Further out on the ledge I stepped before leaping forward, plunging downward keeping my eyes shut and praying I wouldn't encounter any barnyard body parts.

Submerged beneath the surface for a few seconds, I was struck darkness and disorientation. Emerging, I was thrilled to survive and quickly followed my new friends back to the bridge to go again. Over and over, we dove, cannon-balled, catapulted and threw ourselves into the canal. I grew more comfortable and began to experience the kind of inclusion and acceptance I had last glimpsed in sixth grade at Thornell Road. This was great. I couldn't believe how well it was going for my new friends and me. If only the police hadn't interrupted us.

Lined up against the squad car now parked next to the bridge, we looked like the cast of *The Outsiders* except instead of leather jackets; we were all in our undies. In the blink of an eye, I'd gone from school safety to village outlaw, from honor roll student to public enemy number one.

"I'm going to need your names and addresses," the officer said.

"He's just trying to scare us," whispered the boy next to me.

"He's doing a good job," I whispered back, barely able to control my cracking voice.

Waiting to see if the town was going to press charges, my parents did their best to understand why I'd been throwing myself off a canal bridge half-naked in the middle of the day and suggested the need for less radical friends and more appropriate afterschool activities, preferably ones that didn't involve law enforcement. The worst part was realizing the group I'd joined, however briefly, was no longer an option and I'd need to start over in my quest for new friends. Back at school, my mood mirrored the weather as it grew colder and darker each week. Lost and unhappy, I didn't think it was possible, but the cynicism, exclusion and jockeying for popularity all got worse. Someone once said it's always darkest before it's completely black and that's exactly how things went in the fall of 1979 at Barker Road Junior High.

First, without warning, *The Wall* appeared. If a more depressing album than Pink Floyd's *The Wall* is ever released, it will need to come with a padded room and complimentary counseling. Exploring themes of abandonment, abuse, isolation and violence, it presents a uniformly bleak picture of the world and places all figures of authority and especially educators at the center of blame for the horrors of every child's daily life. It is a piece of music that makes you feel like killing yourself. And lucky us, it was on the radio around the clock at a time of life when its messages resonated loudly. Every day, as my classmates and I rode to school, the central Pink Floyd mantra was repeated again and again: *We don't need no education. Teachers, leave them kids alone. You won't get your pudding if you don't eat your meat.* Brick by brick, the forces of evil were surrounding us and there was no escape.

Shortly thereafter, like a club to our collective head, John Lennon was murdered. I learned of his death on *Monday Night Football* from Howard Cosell, an abrasive announcer who saw fit to note Lennon had been shot twice in the back and was dead on arrival at Roosevelt Hospital in New York City. The gruesomeness of it kept me up late that night and the next day a tearful Mr. Whitney spoke of his hero, failing to move the usual suspects who smirked and mocked him even in his moment of ultimate misery. For the rest of us, however, his words meant something. These were the Beatles, a group whose songs we all knew. Infused with a sweetness, innocence and wistfulness, their music, in a small but meaningful way, had shaped us and the way we viewed and met the world. Romantic, uplifting and joyous, Beatles songs were the opposite of *The Wall*. Playing their albums all period, Mr. Whitney explained how much their music meant to him and insisted we do something to honor Lennon. What that would be wasn't clear until a few weeks later when Mr. Whitney, clad in a Beatles t-shirt and his denim vest, called class to order and said he had an announcement.

"We're going to have an all-night dance marathon to raise money for those suffering from muscular dystrophy."

I didn't know why he picked muscular dystrophy but it didn't matter. Staying up all night was a novel concept at age 12 and his announcement sent a ripple of excitement through the classroom even the cynics couldn't deny. The world didn't spin on its axis any differently that day, but I walked out of Mr. Whitney's classroom with some things I didn't have going in: a purpose, a pledge sheet and a reason to believe life wasn't as bad as it seemed.

In turn, my existence at Barker slowly began to get a little better. They were small victories but I met a few nice kids, memorized my locker combination, and got interested in science thanks to Mr. Kokis, a teacher with crazy hair and a crazier voice who liked to listen to the Doobie Brothers while letting his students take turns lighting the Bunsen burner. I still didn't have a close group of friends or the affection of Michelle or anything resembling popularity but as winter retreated and spring advanced, I diligently gathered sponsors and eagerly looked forward to the dance marathon.

The day of the big happening, I tried to do as instructed and nap after school but it was impossible. It was a Friday and I spent the late afternoon and evening figuring out how to look cool and be cool at the dance. By this point in the year, I had learned jeans rather than bone-white corduroys were the way to go if you wanted to position yourself as more Fonzie than Fred Rogers. The hair had to be perfect, too, something that required significant mirror time. Unsurprisingly, I left for the event with a belly full of butterflies and a nagging sense my coiffure and overall appearance weren't quite right.

At school, things began the way every seventh grade dance begins with boys and girls clustered on either side of the gym, moving only to get refreshments before quickly returning to their original spot. Surveying the arrivals, I saw everyone was there including the scum-jumpers, the cynics, Michelle and, of course, Dick. Soon, Mr. Whitney welcomed everyone and explained the rules, reminding us each participant needed to dance continuously all night with brief breaks allowed only for the bathroom or a beverage.

At first it was awkward out on the dance floor. Moving alone, I felt self-conscious. But as the fruit punch flowed and the lights were dimmed, a mirrored disco ball began casting its spell, ameliorating our inhibitions and transporting us to a place we'd never been. The girls got flirtier, the boys got rowdier and the party was on. I positioned myself in the center of the scrum, wildly desirous of full participation. I danced and laughed and shouted with the rest of my classmates, unconcerned about the opinion of others for the first time in a long time. It was easy to see something transformational was taking place. All of us were seizing the opportunity to let out and let go of all the things we'd kept inside during the first year of junior high school. This wasn't just a dance. It was a liberation. And all the confusion, alienation and hurt lifted like a fog that had been surrounding us all year. What remained was joy and a realization we didn't want life to be like *The Wall*. Even Dick was dancing.

Near Midnight, when BTO's *Taking Care of Business* came on, I found myself next to someone I first met in sixth grade but was largely a stranger in seventh due to different homerooms, schedules and bus routes. His name was Chris "Party" Pardi and recognizing each other as reunited allies in this moment, we started shaking our fists in the air in unison to the beat, leaning our arms toward each other in a way that unexpectedly caused others to follow. Before I knew it, Party and I were surrounded by 20 kids all doing the same and all singing as loudly as they possibly could. We continued to look for others to include and in a brief important few minutes, I made a friend and saw myself fitting in as a leader.

At 3:00 a.m., through bleary eyes, I saw Michelle standing alone with a glass of punch as *Stairway to Heaven* came on. I'd been waiting all year for this moment and I didn't hesitate to take advantage of it. With Dick nowhere in sight, I strapped on my suit of armor, mounted my white steed, and asked her to dance. Out on the floor, I held her as tightly as I could and thanked God for eight minute slow songs. I had never been happier. *Should I kiss her or not?* I thought as Led Zeppelin escorted us through their indecipherable world. Conflicted, as the song neared its end, I pulled back from our clinch and looked Michelle straight in the eyes to see if the light was green. It was. But at that moment, I wasn't ready to jump off this bridge so I happily buried my head back into her shoulder. A kiss with Michelle would have to wait.

For the last song of the night, Mr. Whitney instructed everyone to stand holding hands around the perimeter of the gym. Unquestionably affected by the good will and spirit of the evening, nobody hesitated for a moment to do so. Mr. Whitney said he was proud of us. He said we'd done something meaningful. He said we'd never forget this night. He was right. When the Beatles' *All You Need Is Love* played, none could deny it was as appropriate an anthem as any to capture what had transpired. Looking around the gym, with everyone singing and clasping hands, I thought about John Lennon and the impact of his music and Mr. Whitney and the impact of his teaching. Both of them did the same thing. They helped me and all the kids standing in that circle see the good on the other side of *The Wall* and for that we will always be indebted.

2
BRINGING HOME THE IRON

Now I understand why it was so important to my father. He wanted to walk with giants not just up the grocery aisle. He wanted to change the world not just the oil in his car. He wanted to perform beneath the bright lights of Broadway if only one time. So when he heard about the Equitable Family Tennis Challenge, his heart sang like a death row inmate suddenly set free.

If you're like we were when we first heard of dad's quest, you have two pressing questions. What the hell is the Equitable Family Tennis Challenge and why would anyone care about something that sounds so stupid? To answer these questions, we have to go back to 1979. It was the height of America's obsession with tennis. Bjorn Borg and John McEnroe were thrilling crowds with their good cop bad cop routine, Martina Navratilova and Chris Evert wanted to kill each other and Jimmy Connors was running around giving everyone the finger in what we now refer to as the golden days.

Amidst that wholesome milieu, executives at the Equitable Insurance Company had an idea to so big they needed two conference rooms to diagram it. They would sponsor a series of local, regional and sectional family tennis tournaments around the country and bring the sectional winners, all-expenses paid, to New York City during the US Open to play in a national championship tournament alongside the professionals in six categories: husband-wife, brother-sister, father-son, father daughter, mother-son and mother-daughter. Mother-in-law categories were considered but dismissed due to the cost of hurricane coverage.

Dad's first challenge was identifying which category to enter. This required candidly assessing his family's tennis ability and picking the person who would burden him the least on his way to glory. Eyeballing my mother, he saw someone with consistent ground strokes and the world's gentlest serve. On balance, with his raw talent and athleticism making up for her deficiencies, he pictured them hoisting the national championship trophy. My mother on the other hand only pictured my father yelling at her for missing shots at key moments and told him she was out.

Moving on to my sister, my father once again weighed the pros and cons of partnership. An extremely talented singer, musician and actress, Pam was only mildly interested in tennis. More damning, no evidence of a competitive streak had ever reared its head during piano or dance recitals or anywhere else and Dad figured it wasn't likely to do so anytime soon. If she had a history of threatening others with violence during drama camp or school musicals, he might of picked her but as it was he passed.

Dad wanted a fierce, blood-thirsty, remorseless competitor which brought him to me. I was 11-years old and still wearing footy pajamas but my father figured he could toughen me up. When I wasn't busy carrying my blanket, I played little league baseball, soccer and increasingly tennis so dad saw potential. Plus I was his last option and he was desperate.

"I've signed us up for the Equitable," he said as if he'd just crossed the Potomac in a row boat.

"The what?" I asked.

"The Equitable Family Tennis Challenge. You've never heard of it?"

"No. Is that a real thing?" I asked.

"Yes, it's a real thing. Trust me it's a big deal. We're going to play in the father-son category and if we win three tournaments in a row, we're going to New York City to play at the U.S. Open. Isn't it exciting?"

"I won't have to miss Chris Wright's sleepover will I?"

"Of course not. The first tournament is local."

As it turned out, local was as far as we got, losing in the first round of the first tournament to a father-son pair we saw drinking together at the club bar prior to our match, apparently unconvinced we posed a threat. After getting beaten like two party piñatas, we left in shame and Dad drove us home in the rain.

I could tell he was down as he muttered four letter words under his breath and rambled on about lost dreams. The possessed look on his face scared me but mostly I felt sorry for him. He was 41 with all his best years behind him and very little to live for so it was up to me to turn him around.

"Don't worry, Dad. There's always next year," I said.

"I'm not sure. 1980 may not come," he replied forlornly.

"Of course it will. And we'll play this Equitable family tennis doohickey again. I promise."

"It's *not* a doohickey," he said angrily, suddenly coming to life. "It's a *big* deal."

The next year we played the doohickey again and lost in the second round of the local tournament. Although dad threw a ball at our opponents and smashed his racket in the parking lot after the match, he took defeat much better this time and only moped for two weeks. At 12, I was starting to get better and at 42, he was starting to mature. In Dad's mind, we were only a few improvements away from pay dirt.

"You should start lifting weights," he announced to me at dinner one night. "What we need out there is a little more muscle to compete with these 18-year olds."

"Honey, I don't want my little boy lifting weights," my mother said before I could reply. "It could stunt his growth for all we know."

"Nonsense, Alice. We bulk this kid up and he'll be a bulldozer."

"But he's not a piece of construction equipment. He's a child."

"I agree. A child that needs to hit the weight room. That's how we're going to bring home the iron," he added, using his preferred phrase for winning a trophy.

By the time we made our third attempt, I was bigger though not much bulkier. More important, I was better having quit all other sports to concentrate on tennis over the prior year. Dad didn't come out and say it but I could tell he thought this was our last chance to suck the marrow from the Equitable Family Tennis Challenge bone. With the twin anchors of raising a family and full-time employment wrapped firmly around his neck, it was only a matter of time until he lost his ability to stand erect and hold a tennis racket. In turn, I felt the pressure to perform my best. I wouldn't just be playing tennis out there. I'd be saving my father from a meaningless life.

"This is our year, kid," he said as we took the court in the first round of the local tournament and began hitting with our opponents.

Sizing them up, my father set our strategy for the match.

"The dad's got a knee brace so hit everything his way," he instructed me.

"Got it," I said, dutifully preparing to train my fire on the wounded bird.

"Aim for the knee if you can," my father said.

I was learning about killer instinct at the foot of the master and the advice turned out to be good. We executed our plan perfectly and not only won our first match but our second and third, placing us in the finals.

"Do you see the difference in the size of the trophies?" my father asked, pointing to the enormous sterling silver platter awaiting the champions and what looked like a McDonalds' ashtray for the runners-up.

"One's a lot bigger," I acknowledged.

"Keep that in mind when we're out there today," my father said, utilizing yet another tool in his motivational kit.

None of it was necessary, however, as things had changed. The Equitable was no longer a doohickey to me. I cared about winning as much as my father and could now return shots that would have overwhelmed me before, making me a perfect partner to Dad who was not a trained tennis player but a good athlete with fast hands. In our latest configuration, I was the steady one manning the baseline and he was the flashy one roaming the net and poaching relentlessly. Our skills and temperaments aligned, we were the Starsky and Hutch of the father-son circuit.

After winning the local and regional tournaments and two gigantic silver platters, we began dreaming of the only thing in life that mattered: winning an even bigger silver platter. If we captured the sectional tournament, we'd be on our way to the U.S. Open, not as spectators but competitors with full use of the facilities including the practice courts, players' lounge and, of course, the locker room. I could only imagine Bjorn Borg's excitement when he learned he'd be showering with us.

Erie, Pennsylvania, however, still stood between us and New York City. Driving west from our home in Rochester, New York for the final test and settling into a Knights Inn off the thruway, we were two Lancelots in search of an elusive Gwenivere. I could tell Dad was nervous as he paced the hotel room with his racket in hand, practicing his swing and singing *Don't Cry Out Loud*. Nevertheless, once on the court, he was cool as a bowl of chilled gazpacho and we blitzkrieged into the finals without losing a set. Only our final opponents, Don Johnson Sr. and Jr., could stop us now.

In 2001, Don Johnson, Jr. won the Wimbledon men's doubles title at the age of 32. Fortunately for us, when we played him in Erie, he was only 12. However, if we were Starsky and Hutch, the Johnsons were Crockett and Tubbs and from the start the mood on the court was uncomfortably tense with both teams all too aware of the high stakes. The winner would be flying first-class to the Big Apple to compete in a national father-son championship at the U.S. Open. The loser would be going to a Denny's somewhere off the Pennsylvania Turnpike.

Scratching, clawing, chewing, gnawing, the teams fought like rabid dogs competing for a carcass. Every game, every point, every shot mattered as the pregnant wind of momentum blew back and forth across the court, favoring one team only briefly before shifting direction. Finally, match point arrived and we stood on the precipice of greatness, a *carpe diem* moment when a dream long pursued is about to come true or so we thought.

Don Johnson, Sr. spun a serve into my dad's body which he managed to poke back into play. From there, a seemingly endless rally saw the ball traverse the net at least 30 times before Don Johnson, Jr. hit a backhand lob that appeared to be sailing long. Watching it float toward the baseline and anticipating victory, my father shouted "out" as soon as the ball landed. The only problem: the ball was in. Somehow it landed smack on the white painted line. My father hesitated. He wanted to win so much, he saw it out.

"Out!" he repeated with emphasis as if that would make it true.

As aggrieved tennis players usually do when questioning a call, the Johnson duo rushed toward the net and began protesting. I caught eyes with dad and waited for what felt like an eternity for him to speak. But the undisputed leader of our team, the lion who'd been prowling the plains of Erie all afternoon, looked uncertain for the first time so I instinctively stepped in to fill the void.

"Dad, it was good," I said, my words hanging awkwardly in the air, my face on the crest of crestfallen.

"Are you sure?" he asked.

"Yes," I said.

He nodded and announced the corrected call to the Johnsons, sending them back to their stations and diffusing the situation. I felt uncomfortable overruling my dad but relieved he'd done the right thing and soon enough a second opportunity to end things presented itself. After three years and two disappointing failures, we were one tantalizing point away from Flushing Meadows. Surely the gods would smile on us this time and send us on our way to the paved promised land in Queens where the greatest tennis players in the world are crowned and immortalized. Not so fast.

By now, each team's inherent suspicion of the other had grown into a genuine hatred and as it bubbled up beneath the quaking lid of the pressure cooker in which we all sat, I couldn't help but revel in the moment. How many kids get to take the field with their father? Not many I guessed, certain I'd never forget the experience.

Another intense point ensued and eventually ended when Don Sr. hit a missile past my head. I turned in time to see it clip the sideline and hear my father make another wrong call.

"Out!" he shouted confidently before walking toward me to partake in the traditional post-match partner handshake.

Here we go again, I thought as the Johnsons stormed the net cursing and pointing fingers at us.

"Dad, it hit the line," I said, amidst the uproar.

"Dammit!" he blurted, unable to muffle his frustration. "It looked wide."

My father taught me to be honest and now he was reaping what he'd sown much to his dismay. So on we went, the match teetering like a Jenga tower. A single mistake and all our hopes of going to New York, of sharing the stage with John McEnroe, of showering with Bjorn Borg, would crash to Earth and shatter irreparably. Ten minutes later, three hours into the match, a third opportunity to finish what we'd begun in

1979 was upon us and this time we would not be denied. After rifling a flat serve up the middle, my father rushed the net and put away a weak return from Don Jr. It was over. I leapt into my father's arms and we celebrated as if we'd won the lottery.

"This is the best day of my life," dad exclaimed as I returned to my feet and we jumped up and down.

"Better than the day I was born?" I asked.

"By a country mile," he beamed unapologetically. "I'm so happy."

By the time we boarded a 737 bound for LaGuardia a few weeks later to go play in the national championship, there wasn't a bottle big enough to contain dad's optimism.

"There isn't a team in the world that can beat us," he said, digging into his pack of peanuts and signaling the stewardess to bring him another Tanqueray and tonic.

Dad had never taken a tennis lesson in his life and I was a five foot two inch 13-year old so we had no business thinking we could win at Flushing Meadows but details like that never slowed down my father.

"After we win the nationals, I'm sure there's an international championship. Of course, we'll have to pull you out of school to train for it."

"Sounds good to me," I said, accepting my father's words as the gospel truth and looking forward to dropping out of school.

"We may even have to move to Europe for a few months," he added.

"Really? You think mom will go for that?"

"Of course, but do me a favor and don't mention it yet."

I paused to contemplate the possibilities and comprehend the unfolding events of my life.

"Dad, why is all this so important to you?" I asked.

"Good question," he said, taking a sip of his drink. "But you won't understand until you get older."

Dad did me the favor of not explaining life's harder lessons that day. He knew in time I'd learn certain things happen to you and those around you as you age and although a lot of these things are good, some of them are not. When friends and family members get divorced or sick or laid off you feel pain and confront your own vulnerability and mortality at the same time, which makes those moments when you're freely using your talents to reach for things beyond your ordinary grasp, like giant silver platters, so exhilarating.

In New York, the Equitable put us up at the Waldorf and held a cocktail reception for all participants on the top floor of the hotel. Everybody there was ebullient, only half-believing they'd gotten this far. Champagne fizzed, hors d'oeuvres circulated and championship spoils for each of the six tournament categories sat prominently on a raised platform in the center of the room, only these weren't silver platters, they were six foot high trophies that looked like replicas of the Empire State Building.

"There's ours," Dad said, pointing to the father-son award. "I'll have to build a new case to hold it when we get home."

That night, courtesy of our hosts, we dined at The Palm, a Second Avenue steakhouse founded in the 1920s that evoked the kind of crowded, noisy, glamorous New York I had imagined. My father remembered the restaurant from his childhood and said my grandfather, an advertising executive, took clients there to down martinis, devour Porterhouses and plan their next conquest. Surrounded by caricatures of Batman, Popeye and other heroes drawn by cartoonists from King

Features Syndicate, the eatery's earliest patrons, we did a version of the same. Feasting on steaks and pieces of cheesecake the size of shoeboxes, we plotted the downfall of our first round opponents, a team from Texas, as if we ruled the world.

The next day, we arrived at the National Tennis Center in a chauffeured limousine. Flashing player badges issued to us by the Equitable, we strutted across the U.S. Open grounds like celebrities, two cocks of the walk ready to inflict damage on anyone who dared to get between us and the winner's trophy.

Inside the players' lounge, the drab interior and stale odor did nothing to dull our competitive drive as we milled among anonymous pros and anxiously awaited our start time. Before long, our names were called and we were ushered to one of the many outer courts to play. We'd made it. Prime time at the U.S. Open.

The promised Texas twosome, already on court, introduced themselves as Dustin and Doyle Cooper. Our first task as always was to figure out who was the weaker player, something that usually made itself obvious but was less clear here.

"Looks like we're up against a couple of cowboys," Dad said to me as walked back to the baseline to warm-up. "Let's show them how we do things here in New York."

The son was one of those 18-year olds my father feared due to his size and strength. A foot taller and fifty pounds heavier than me, Doyle had the potential to cause a mismatch.

"That kid is huge," Dad observed once he got a better look at him.

"He's not the first older kid we've faced," I said.

"I know but for God's sake, I saw him shaving together in the locker room before the match. He looks like he's 25. I may have to ask for a driver's license."

"Dad, don't do that. We can handle him."

"You're right but let's hit everything to the father. I saw him applying some ointment to his groin before we started."

"Got it. Hit toward the guy with the bad groin."

As it turned out, Dustin and Doyle were equally good players, both with big first serves, powerful volleys and perfectly functional groins. On the big stage of Flushing, however, they were nervous and we managed to win a tight first set 6-4.

"We're on our way," Dad said to me, our collective confidence soaring. "There isn't a team alive that can stop us."

"You know it," I said, taking out a mortgage on my father's irresistible rhetoric.

Unfortunately, all of our excitement proved premature. In the second set, the Coopers refused to relinquish the net and Dad and I found ourselves scrambling to stay even. Making uncharacteristic errors, we fell further and further behind until it was over and the match transformed from a wonderful opportunity to a painful memory.

Sitting on the sidelines, our bowed heads soaked in sweat, we couldn't believe it.

"I'm sorry," my father said, using a word that didn't come easily to him.

"Why?" I asked, genuinely perplexed about his apology.

"I missed too many shots."

"We both missed shots, Dad."

"I missed more,"

"It's okay."

"I let you down," he said.

"No, you didn't."

"But we lost."

"Dad, we lost. But we're here. We made it to the big time. We shared a locker room with Johnny Mac."

"You're right," he said, visibly brightened by my charity. "If we start training next week, we'll be ready to give this thing another shot next year."

"That's the spirit," I said.

"I know we can win this thing."

'Of course we can," I said.

"Because when we're on our game, there isn't another team in the world that can touch us."

"Dad, I couldn't agree more."

3
ROCK AND ROLL

Seventh grade was a year of firsts. Some good: my first dance, my first French kiss, my first real girlfriend. Some bad: my first trip to detention, my first zit, my first real break-up with the above mentioned first real girlfriend. More monumental than any of it, however, was my first rock and roll concert.

This wasn't just any concert mind you. We're talking Foreigner at the Rochester, New York War Memorial. Does it get any bigger than that? Not to a 12-year old. So when I heard they were coming to town, I pleaded with my parents to let me go.

"I'm not sure that's a good idea," my mother said.

"Why not?" I asked.

"Wasn't someone stabbed at the last concert?"

"Yes, but nobody died," I said.

Today, the War Memorial is known as the Blue Cross Blue Shield Arena, a perfectly pleasant but antiseptic environment replete with corporate signage and overpriced food where you're more likely to see sushi than a scuffle between patrons. But in 1979, the

HIGH SCHOOL DANCE

War Memorial was a drug-laden den of dangerous outlaws, and those were just the guys taking tickets.

"What if we go with you?" my father suggested.

"Dad, I'm not a baby anymore."

"I know but Mom and I would feel better this way. Tell you what. You can bring a couple friends. You'll hardly know we're there."

This was a compromise but one that came with great opportunity so I accepted it. I was ready for my shot at danger, something I'd never had. My older sister said everyone at the concert would be carrying, holding or packing and though I had no idea what she meant, it sounded wonderfully corrupting. Best of all, when word got out I had Foreigner tickets and could invite two lucky classmates to join me, I would go from a jester-in-waiting with no close friends to King of the Seventh Grade. Of course, word about my parents coming along would be kept quiet at all costs.

For those of us at Barker Road Junior High, Foreigner held a place of high honor like Docksiders or Magic Shell. The lead singer was native son, Lou Gramm, who left Rochester years before as Louis Grammatico and was now returning with a short name but a long list of hit songs, all of which we knew by heart. He was proof someone from our city could hit it big doing something legal and any one of us could be next.

The band's music stirred something within me. My pubescent mind may have been muddled, but I was pretty sure their latest hit, *Dirty White Boy*, was about something other than getting muddy. More perplexing, the cover of their latest album, *Head Games*, showed an exotic-looking woman in a short skirt sitting backwards in a urinal. For the life of me, I couldn't figure out how she ended up in the men's room but I was hopeful someone would kindly redirect her.

The show sold out almost immediately, but somehow my parents secured five tickets. Armed with my two spares, I shamelessly lorded them over my classmates each day in the cafeteria, encouraging them to curry favor with me by any means necessary. This mostly meant extra desserts, tater tots and pizza, all of which never tasted better. Everybody wanted to go to the show; everybody but Eddie Mercer, a scrawny kid who considered himself the arbiter of what was good and bad.

"Foreigner sucks," Eddie scowled every time the subject came up, relishing his role as the sole hold-out.

"Who do you like? Foghat?" I asked.

"I bet he likes the Village People or maybe Peaches and Herb," our tablemate John Conners said, issuing the biggest insults he could think of at the time.

What's wrong with Peaches and Herb? I thought, making a mental note to hide my *Shake Your Groove Thing* 45 when I got home that day.

"Have any of you ever heard of The Who?" Eddie said. "Now, that's a *real* rock and roll band."

"Maybe so, but they're never coming to the War Memorial and Foreigner is," I pointed out, staying mum about my errant love of Peaches and Herb.

Eventually, after assessing their fitness and fealty, I deigned Kenny Patrick and Tim Collins worthy of attendance and invited them to the show, scheduled for late October. Kenny, the world's biggest *Star Wars* fan, confessed to the recent insertion of tubes in his ears but promised the force was with him while Tim, a redhead who said he was ranked fifth on the east coast in racquetball, satisfied me he had no health issues. Everything was aligned perfectly for a trip to rock and roll heaven. Unfortunately, a week before the concert, the part about my parents serving as chaperones became public knowledge at school. Apparently, one mother called another and now I was in for it.

"Hey O'Dwyer, I hear your mommy and daddy are going to be babysitting you guys at the Foreigner concert," Eddie Mercer teased with sinister glee in his voice. "Will they be bringing a diaper bag?" he shouted across the cafeteria.

"Shut-up, Eddie," I replied, trying my best to deflect the attention and praying he wouldn't learn of my collection of Village People albums.

"Make sure mommy packs your pacifier," Eddie added, cackling at his own cleverness.

With my tail tucked between my legs, I shuffled through the lunch line trying to ignore the incoming barbs and turn my focus toward my ongoing shop project, welding two strips of metal into an enormous F in tribute to my favorite band. Nothing anyone said was going to dim my enthusiasm for the upcoming event or welding for that matter.

The night of the show, I got ready by singing in front of my mirror pretending to be Lou Gramm. Belting out big ones like *Hot Blooded* and *Cold as Ice*, I wondered why the band was so temperature sensitive but figured it had something to do with getting older. My grandmother was always asking for an afghan and these guys looked like they were getting up there.

In the car, my parents put on 96.5 WCMF and Kenny, Tim and I contorted ourselves to *Blue Morning Blue Day* at a decibel level exceeded only by our excitement. Making our way to downtown Rochester and seeing the surrounding environment through the car window, I was suddenly glad my parents were with me, a sentiment that only grew when we entered the War Memorial.

Inside the concrete corridors, countless people with long hair, tattoos and sleeveless leather vests made me feel entirely out of place, not to mention the pervasive smell surrounding us. If I hadn't been so naïve, I would have known I was coming face to face with America's recreational drug habit, but not knowing anything about marijuana I speculated concessions had overcooked some kind of awful food.

"What is that smell?" I asked.

"I'm not sure," my dad said, shielding those in his charge as well as my mother, from reality. "Could be a dead animal," he added. "They hold rodeos here sometimes."

"That must have been some rodeo," Tim observed.

In our seats, we felt the unique, anticipatory energy that exists in the minutes prior to a rock show as the War Memorial crowd teetered on the edge of delirium. Like a tsunami, suddenly it was upon us. The stadium went dark, the cheers became deafening and shadowy figures ran on to the stage. When the lights came back up, there was Foreigner launching into *Long, Long, Way from Home*, an apropos song as I inhaled pot smoke and contemplated what kind of tattoo to get.

Shaking our seats in the rafters and sending vibrations through my body, the music's power and volume were far beyond anything I'd known. Sure, my dad had cranked it up in the car on occasion, but the station wagon stereo had never threatened me with permanent hearing loss. This was different and I realized I was experiencing rock and roll the way it was meant to be for the first time, and right then I decided I loved it -

HIGH SCHOOL DANCE

even more than Docksiders, Magic Shell or Peaches and Herb.

In between songs, the crowd held Bic lighters in the air and went back to their smoking. It was then, following a thunderous version of *Double Vision*, the hazy wheels on my rolling fantasy began to come off. First, the burly, bearded man sitting next to my mother unrolled a piece of tinfoil uncovering what I took to be tobacco. Placing a pinch in the small curved bowl at the end of a strange looking pipe, he proceeded to light it, inhale it and offer it up to my mom. *So silly. Doesn't he know women don't smoke pipes?* She politely declined but her body language told me she was extremely uncomfortable and caused me to rethink what was in the tinfoil. 'Did that guy offer my mom drugs?'

I was wrapping my head around the possibility when I noticed Kenny holding his ears and writhing in pain.

"What's wrong?" I said, raising my voice.

"My tubes. Something's going on with my tubes."

When Kenny told me his doctor put tubes in his hear, I pictured large rubber hoses.

"What's wrong with them?"

"I don't know but my ears are killing me. The music's too loud. I want to go home," Kenny said, now in tears.

"Now? But the show's only half way over," I said in disbelief.

As my mother tried to comfort Kenny, I looked over at Tim for moral support. Surely he wouldn't want to leave. He was almost as big a Foreigner fan as I was. Tim, however, was sound asleep, his head resting on my father's shoulder.

"Tim, wake up!" I shouted. "You're missing the show."

It was no use. With Kenny crying, Tim snoring and my mother fending off drug dealers, my father made an executive decision.

"We're going home," he announced.

"But, dad, they haven't even played *Dirty White Boy* yet," I protested.

"I don't care if they haven't played *The Star-Spangled Banner*," my father replied. "We're going."

Leaving mid-show, I felt like a loser but time quickly lent perspective and by Monday at school with a ringing still in my head, I reported to my classmates we attended the greatest musical happening since Woodstock. Eddie Mercer continued to insist Foreigner sucked, but I knew better. What other band could blow the tubes out of one kid's ears while putting another to sleep? Talk about versatility and a testament to their greatness. These days when Lou Gramm and the boys come on the radio I turn it up, sing along and fondly remember my first time. Long live Foreigner. Long live rock and roll.

4
HEROES

My mother's intentions were good. Honestly. She didn't know from tennis. So after two lessons, she signed me up for a tournament and sent me to the happiest place on Earth: the junior circuit. Sure, reasonable people could disagree whether entering me in the advanced category represented a mother's overconfidence or child abuse, but no way she knew she was relegating me to a place where souls regularly go to die and the obnoxiousness of the kids is eclipsed only by the lunacy of the parents.

Arriving at Rochester Institute of Technology's shade-free courts, I suspected I was over my head immediately. Most of the players had matching tennis outfits, fancy racket bags and what appeared to be coaches. I had one racket, cut-off shorts, no bag and my mother, who knew as much about sports as a squirrel knew about science. Still, the whole thing promised to be good summer fun and a great way to get a head start on skin cancer.

My opponent was a midget. Not a circus midget or little person with their own reality TV show, but a short, skinny kid whose racket looked like an oversized snowshoe in his teeny hands. Pulling me aside, my mother gave me a few key tips.

"This guy's tiny. He should be no problem, honey. No problem at all."

Coming from a woman who was five feet tall in heels, the words made sense. After all, who better than my mom to size up a short person.

"Are you sure, Mom?"

"Of course. He looks like he can barely lift the racket. You may want to take it easy on him," she continued, pumping me up like a prize-fighter about to enter the ring.

I nodded and prepared to destroy this kid and his dreams. I looked at the boys' 10 and under draw sheet but disregarded the number one placed next to my new enemy's name. I assumed it was his shoe size as opposed to his seeding, the number that tells you where a player is expected to finish in the tournament based on his current ranking. Like my mother, I didn't know from tennis either.

The tournament director called our last names loudly and up to the starter's table we stepped. At four foot three, I towered over Sean Carvey like Everest over a doomed climber. I actually felt sorry for him as we received our balls and court assignment and the director wished us luck. *He's gonna need it*, I thought, entering the fenced courts for what would no doubt be a quick cage match.

I was right on one account. It was quick. Before I could tie my Stan Smiths, I was down five games to zero. Turned out size wasn't everything especially on a tennis court with Sean Carvey. The kid was a perfectly-timed ball machine, hitting winners from both wings, passing me at will and rarely missing a shot. In contrast, my game was comprised exclusively of two kinds of shots: forced errors and unforced errors. My solution was hitting harder, a new strategy that immediately resulted in a third kind of shot: spectacular errors.

As Carvey's lead and my frustration grew in equal measure, I reached for the last tool in the shed: good old-fashioned racket chucking. If I had learned anything during my two lessons and my brief but illustrative time on the junior circuit, it was the right and duty of every player to start throwing their racket around violently in disgust when things went south. So after losing the first set, I really got into it and began launching my racket like the space shuttle every time I lost a point. By the time I went to shake hands with Carvey after a 6-0, 6-0 drubbing, my aluminum Head Edge looked like a piece of twisted modern art.

Mom and I didn't speak on the ride home. We were both beset by tennis-related toxic shock syndrome. Arriving at our house, she commenced the Herculean task of unfolding my racket while I staggered off to my room mumbling about the need for a third or perhaps fourth lesson before taking Carvey on again. As I looked back, I had a lot to think about. Carvey was so small and so quiet. Talk about making me look bad. He never even chucked his racket. How could this happen? How could I lose?

A week later, a newspaper article on the front of the sports section answered my questions. Underneath a large picture of Carvey hitting one of his nuclear forehands, I learned he was a wunderkind, the best player for his age in the whole area and one of the best in the state. Now, it all made sense. I'd been up against a ringer, a freak of nature. I didn't need to feel so bad about myself.

I had an excuse. What a relief. In celebration I cut out the article and taped it to my bedroom wall where Carvey joined a pantheon of my childhood heroes ranging from KISS to Ziggy to Captain and Tennille. My tennis career could have happily ended right there, but as I stared at Carvey's picture on my wall, a wire within me tripped.

Something was definitely different. Like my other heroes, I admired and envied Sean Carvey and wanted to be like him. I also wanted to kick his ass, however, and I couldn't recall feeling the same way about KISS or Ziggy or frankly anyone else adorning my wall. Emerging from my solitude, I asked my mother to sign me up for more lessons and more tournaments.

"Are you sure?" she asked.

Witnessing the beating I took, she understandably questioned whether subjecting me to more of the same was a good thing.

"I'm sure."

"Okay, but no more racket chucking," she said, holding up the still-mangled piece of metal I'd abused.

"One chuck per match?" I trial-ballooned, knowing how satisfying it was to let it fly.

"No chucking."

With the ground rules established, my assault on Mount Carvey began. To put it mildly, the climbing required more oxygen than I expected. At first, I had it all figured out. According to the newspaper article, Carvey played at the Tennis Club of Rochester a/k/a TCR so I decided that's where I'd play. My parents were good sports going into debt to sign me up for a membership and group lessons, and I quickly became a club rat, spending all my time participating in the groups and playing pick-up matches with anyone who breathed. TCR had a junior challenge ladder where you could propose a duel to the person above you and take their spot if you won, a Darwinian arrangement I couldn't get enough of as I set my sights on Sean.

Of course, what I hadn't anticipated was Carvey and I would become friends. Far from acting like an enemy, he was kind to me and before I knew it, we were hanging around together. He even invited me to his house for lunch which was walking distance from the club. What a rotten trick. How was I going to stay motivated to annihilate this guy if he kept hitting me with hospitality? Nevertheless, I took him up on his offer and got the shock of my life when he showed me the pristine tennis court situated amidst a grove of trees behind his house. Holy Vitas Gerulaitis! Beating Sean Carvey was going to be a lot harder than I thought.

"We need to install a court," I informed my parents that night at dinner.

"A what?" my dad asked.

"A tennis court. Sean Carvey has his own court. Now, I've been outside and I've found the perfect spot. We'll have to move part of the driveway but it's all doable."

Without missing a beat, my father got up from the table and motioned me to come with him.

"Let me show you something," he said.

Leading me down the basement stairs, he came to a stop in a particularly congested area full of porch furniture, boxed Christmas decorations and what otherwise looked like a graveyard of things we'd never use again but couldn't bear to throw out.

"What are we doing down here?" I asked, genuinely perplexed.

"Welcome to your new tennis court," he said.

"Are you kidding?"

"If we move a few of these things, you'll have a perfect wall to hit against."

"How do you move a hot water heater?" I asked, observing the permanent plumbing clearly not going anywhere.

"You don't. You'll have to hit around it. Think how accurate you're going to get."

"So we're not getting a real tennis court?"

"No, we're not."

With Carvey ensconced in his own personal Wimbledon, I settled into my basement each night. If I could swing at the ball, avoid the water heater and hit the small patch of concrete just above the tool bench, I could occasionally get a rally going. Errant shots regularly hit light bulbs forcing me to flee from showers of broken glass and endure shouts of 'what the hell are you doing down there?' but personal safety and scorn are of no concern when you're on a quest.

Next, I asked my mother for the membership fee to join the United States Tennis Association, which in turn sent me a booklet listing all of the tournaments in the region.

"We need to go to Binghamton next weekend," I announced.

"What for?" asked my dad.

Today it's commonplace today for kids to travel for sporting events, but not so much in the 1970s. Except when the Bad News Bears went to Japan, everything was local and parents needed convincing to drive more than a half hour for anything.

"That's where the next tournament is," I said.

"Why can't you play a tournament right here in Rochester?" my father asked.

"I can, but the next one's in Binghamton and Sean Carvey's going to be there. I can't beat him if I don't play him. This is my dream, dad."

"I got it. I just didn't realize the dream involved weekends in Binghamton. When I was your age, we went down to the duck pond and threw on our skates."

If my father knew the truth, he might have called the dream off right then and there because Binghamton was only the beginning. Growing up, he'd played hockey, football, baseball, whatever was in season, lettering eight times in high school. But this was the dawn of sports specialization and the days of going down to the duck pond with your skates were over. Tennis was a year round endeavor and tournaments never ceased, taking us up and down the New York State thruway over and over again. I realized I would need to abandon all other sports and gradually let baseball, soccer and skiing fade before disappearing from my schedule.

"When's the off-season for this sport?" he wondered aloud.

"There isn't one, dad."

"You gotta be joking."

Expenses added up with lessons, shoes, rackets, travel, entry fees a dozen other costs, and my father understandably questioned the need for it all on more than one occasion, especially when I lost, something I did a lot.

"I'm spending half my paycheck on your tennis! Don't you want to play little league?" he asked, testing the limits of my devotion in the face of failure and silently hoping to be freed from this budget-busting endeavor.

"No," I said, resolute in my cause.

Truth told, despite my doggedness, after a period of complete dedication I was frustrated. Even with all the lessons, challenge matches and hours I spent hitting around the water heater in our basement, I hadn't caught Carvey, who regularly obliterated me in Buffalo, skewered me in Schenectady and asphyxiated me in Albany.

"It's going to take some time," my mother assured me.

"Can I start chucking my racket again?" I asked.

"No. You just need to keep playing him," she said.

"There's a tournament in Utica in two weeks," I enthused.

"I can hardly wait," my father said in more muted fashion.

After two years, I was still losing to Carvey but the matches were no longer a source of family embarrassment. We became doubles partners and good friends, leaving me in the ongoing, uncomfortable position of trying to out-do someone I respected and liked. Even as I pursued him, Sean was still one of my heroes and a model of sportsmanship. He was also principally responsible for my first trophy when he carried us to the boys' 12 and under doubles championship at Sedgwick Farm in Syracuse, where we each received silver bowls, an event that gave me self-confidence and gave my mother something to polish for the next decade.

By the time I turned 13, I had been chasing Sean Carvey for almost four years and had never beaten him, but the intensity of our matches had grown dramatically. Our skill sets were comparable now and I began to push him to the brink of defeat. Instead of straight set victories, every match went three sets and ended in agonizingly close scores. I was still on the losing end, but the possibility of beating him became real and drove me harder to get better. Time after time, he nicked me at the finish line until; finally, at a tournament in Rochester, it happened. I beat him.

Somewhere in a shoebox, I have a picture of it. The two of us immediately after the match, my face one big smile, my trophy held up prominently, his face in tears, his trophy hidden down by his legs. The final score was 3-6, 6-3, 7-5 and I was ecstatic. All the heartbreaking near misses were suddenly worth the pain of finishing second so many times. The thrill lasted a few hours but before long a funny thing happened. I felt sorry for Sean and I felt guilty about beating him. I remembered the first time we played and imagined how difficult it had to be from his end, having someone constantly trying to take what was yours for so long.

I never lost to Sean Carvey again. We played several more times but, within a year or two, I noticed he wasn't entering many tournaments and by the time I reached the 16 and under division, he had largely vanished. I didn't understand until word got around his mother had run off to South Carolina, his parents had divorced and he'd lost interest in tennis. To that point in my life, I had given little thought to the impact of divorce on children but now found myself contemplating it, feeling empathy for Sean and realizing how lucky I was to be spared his painful reality. Given the individual, isolating nature of tennis and the tremendous family support needed to enable a child to thrive in competition, it was easy for me to understand why he stepped away. For all of us players, it was understood and accepted we'd be alone on the court. However, nobody warned us we might be alone when we got off.

To this day, I owe Sean Carvey a lot. He set a benchmark for me and was always a friend in spite of our rivalry. Sometimes your heroes disappoint you. Sean Carvey never did.

5
FAILURE

Mr. Whitney's feel-good charity dance marathon at the end of seventh grade should have been enough to propel me into eighth grade with positive momentum and a warm fuzzy feeling of inclusion. But after a summer away from school, I arrived back at Barker Road Junior High in the fall feeling as displaced as ever. Lost somewhere between social groups, identities and bad haircuts, I knew eighth grade was going to be hard but I had no idea a year of intense and unyielding failure awaited me. Boy was I in for it.

It started with my trumpet. After lugging it around for five years, I was looking for the perfect moment to quit and believed I'd found it until my father, who'd purchased the instrument on an installment plan and fancied me the next Louis Armstrong, inconveniently informed me it was paid off and forever mine. I shouldn't have felt guilty quitting at such an inopportune time. After all, it was my father who pushed me toward the trumpet due to his fervent belief the guitar led to a life in subway stations playing Peter, Paul and

Mary songs for rent money. But being the dutiful son I was, I did feel guilty and resigned myself to another year in the band. *This won't be so bad*, I thought, settling into position as fifth trumpet out of five in my assigned row. Resignation to this fate, however, did not last long as I emptied my spit valve and began to scheme.

The band leader, Miss Kramer, never smiled, wielding her baton with a look on her face like she was undergoing a colonoscopy. She took her job seriously and deserved more respect from me, but I was determined to get kicked out and figured it wouldn't take much of an infraction to do so. My quiet rebellion started with what I called playing against the grain. Also known as being an immature jerk, it involved playing *When the Saints Go Marching In* while the rest of the band played something else. Positive that doing this repeatedly would elicit Miss Kramer's condemnation and earn me an ejection from class, I was stunned when my insubordination went ignored. The band was so bad and its muddled sound so cacophonous, my actions had no effect. I had never rebelled before and apparently I wasn't very good at it. Score one for Miss Kramer and call in the cliché about temporary insanity because my next gambit upped the ante considerably.

The boy who'd always gone to church, never spoke back to adults and continually did the right thing, started skipping his weekly private lesson with Miss Kramer scheduled during school hours. Whenever it was time to go, I made myself scarce, heading for the cafeteria, library or nurse's office. For whatever reason, I didn't care about the consequences and embraced the frightening thrill of daring the authorities to come down on me. Somehow though, they didn't. Despite all my evasion, nobody appeared to be paying attention, and once again I marveled at my failed insurrection.

Nobody *said* anything or *did* anything. It was downright maddening. Couldn't these people see I was a troubled youth in need of discipline?

The answer to this riddle arrived with my first quarter report card. Usually opening and reading this document was a pleasurable experience for my parents, so it was somewhat jarring to hear my father commanding me to his home office with anger in his voice. It was common knowledge in our household that a trip to Dad's domain was never a good thing but I was so accustomed to praise for my school work, I didn't realize what I was facing.

"What's up, Daddy-O?" I asked, a little too casually for my own good as I entered his office.

"What's up? Your report card is what's up."

"Another good one?" I asked, my voice absent of confidence.

"What the hell happened in band?"

"What do you mean?"

"You got an F."

"I did?"

"Yes, look here," he said, pointing to the paper. "How does anyone get an F in band? Did you assault the teacher?"

"Not exactly, Dad."

"Then what happened? You've never gotten an F."

"Maybe it's a misprint," I said.

"I don't think so. All your grades are down."

I loved my parents and felt free to tell them anything but I couldn't tell my father I wanted to quit the trumpet. I'd never quit anything in my life.

"I can tell you one thing. You're going to be playing a lot less tennis until these grades come up," he said, threatening the one thing I truly cared about.

Over the prior two years, I had fallen in love with tennis and within the four corners of the court, I escaped from the alienation I was experiencing at school. My mother knew this and intervened on my behalf, miraculously buying me a reprieve. If I promised to turn things around in band and elsewhere by the end of the next quarter, I could keep playing. I breathed a sigh of relief, winded like I'd just blown a long, off-key note. Life, however, was about to get more complicated.

Some of my fellow eighth graders experimenting with alcohol and pot, but I was afraid to try either. I knew was those things caused you to lose control and, given the rudderless feelings I was already enduring, I saw no reason to add to them. I resolved to avoid any situation where I would be subjected to six packs of beer, hastily rolled joints and the pressure to partake, an altogether unrealistic proposition that only a naïve 13-year old could entertain. Naturally, it wasn't long before reality intruded.

My parents planned a family trip to Canada to celebrate New Year's Eve. The Oban Inn in Niagara-on-the-Lake Ontario was the kind of place my father loved: formal, tradition-bound and possessed of an expansive bar area, enormous hearth and baby grand piano, perfect for him to spontaneously entertain a crowd with his 1950s' rock and roll repertoire. Established in 1824, the inn was a place where people still celebrated the new year with a nostalgic reverence evidenced by their attire and spirit. Plaid kilts, ball gowns, tuxedoes and toasts to the Queen of England were commonplace and in the midst of the merriment you couldn't help but feel like you'd stumbled onto a Frank Capra movie set only this was real. I wasn't sure what to make of men in skirts but clearly something special was afoot.

Dressed in our best, we had a wonderful dinner of wild game shot by the chef and settled into the long and somewhat chaotic hours leading up to the new year with people coming and going from the bar area paying little attention to their teenage kids, drinking and relaxing in the festive setting. It was then, with my father joyously positioned behind the piano surrounded by dozens of Canadians singing *Earth Angel*, that I noticed my sister, Pam, and the friend she was allowed to invite along, Amy, were gone. Wondering if they'd gone back up to our room, I borrowed a key from my mother and went in search of them.

Upon entering our small suite, the first thing I noticed was giggling coming from the bathroom and a strange smell. Moving closer, I could see they were smoking something and when my sister saw me, she was not happy.

"Hey, get out of here!" she shouted.

"What are you guys doing?" I asked, fairly certain I knew what was going on.

"What's it look like?"

"Are you smoking pot?"

"Yes. And you better not tell mom and dad," Pam said.

"You're going to get us kicked out of Canada," I said, picturing a Royal Mountie bursting through the door on a horse at any minute.

"I am not."

Although my sister was only doing what many 15-year olds were doing at the time, experimenting with one of life's temptations, I felt a deep disappointment accompanied by fear. The levee that kept me separate from drugs had been breached in a way that was unexpected and unwanted and I rushed from the room, certain if I stood there much longer I would turn into Cheech and Chong's marijuana mascot.

I didn't say a word to my parents about what I witnessed in Ontario but my relationship with my sister changed that day. Instead of seeing her smoking as a small forgivable offense, I condemned Pam as if she'd murdered someone. My decision to resist things like alcohol and pot may have been well-reasoned but it made me unbearably self-righteous and judgmental. In the weeks and months that followed, we argued about this topic endlessly and I repeatedly called her a loser, something that cleaved our friendship. Before long, I was more alone than ever, walking the halls of Barker Road like a zombie with a trumpet case full of worries. Little did I know my biggest failures were still to come.

Concerned about my grades and my father's threat to end my tennis career, I felt pressure to ace every class and was especially concerned about science where Ms. Barnes administered pop quizzes with alarming regularity. I had been keeping up pretty well but as the year wore on, my constant worrying made me vulnerable to dark forces and right on time they arrived.

It was a day like any other in science class. We took our seats and Ms. Barnes announced we were having a surprise test. Everybody groaned and got out their pencils, readying for the onslaught. Although I wasn't as prepared as I would have liked, I took the test and handed it in, certain I had done okay. I walked out of class relieved it was over when I was suddenly accosted by Will Simmons, my lab partner.

Will Simmons wasn't the best science student in the world, which is a nice way of saying he thought Isaac Newton was a type of cookie.

"I've got the answer key," he whispered forcefully.
"What?"

"The test we just took. I saw the answer key on Barnes' desk and I swiped it."

"Are you crazy?"

"All we have to do is go back in and change our answers."

I had never cheated in my life and had no good reason to do so now but the power of suggestion prevailed and before I knew it I was back in Ms. Barnes' darkened room, rifling through the pile of tests on her desk and sneaking off with mine while Will grabbed his and retreated with me to the boys' bathroom. Down on our hands and knees a few feet from the toilets, we placed the key between us on the floor and furiously reviewed our papers as the stench of urine and Lysol enveloped us.

Will began erasing wildly as most of his answers were wrong but mine were mostly right so while he replaced quite a lot, I changed three answers to raise my grade from an 88 to a 94. In a blur, we returned the newly marked tests to the pile in the classroom and went our separate ways, two cat burglars seemingly in the clear.

It was a Friday so I had plenty of time to think about what I'd done over the weekend and when Monday arrived, I shuddered at the prospect of attending school. I couldn't believe I had cheated and the more I contemplated my misdeed, the more certain I was I'd be caught, a prediction that appeared to be coming true when Ms. Barnes began class.

"I'm afraid I have some extremely upsetting news," she said, putting Will and me into full blown panic. "It's come to my attention that some of you cheated on Friday's test."

I knew we'd get caught. I knew it. Why did I ever listen to Simmons and his stupid plan?

"For the students who took the test fairly, rest assured I'm going to get to the bottom of this. I cannot tell you how disappointed I am. When you cheat, you cheat your classmates and me and you cheat yourself out of an education."

As the days went by, I nervously waited for the hammer to hit me in the face but it didn't and after a week, I pulled Will aside.

"What happened?" I asked him, making sure we were alone.

"I got nailed."

"You did?"

"Barnes gave me a zero on the test. I guess I shouldn't have given myself a perfect score. She said it wasn't believable given my 68 average."

"Yeah, I guess not," I said, commiserating as best I could. "Did my name come up at all?" I asked, wincing in anticipation of the answer.

"No and don't worry. I'll take the fall."

"Thanks, Will." I said, unable to muster any other words or the bravery to confess.

Unlike Will, I was without honor. My sister wasn't the loser. I was. An F student in band, the world's worst brother, a cheat and a coward, I didn't think I could sink any lower, but once again I was wrong.

Leslie Barnett was a girl in my class I knew about but didn't know. Among the first to discover the impact bleach has on your hair, she stuck out not only because of her platinum locks but also due to her clothes and attitude. Continually experimenting with her wardrobe like a wannabe Madonna, she had an energy that radiated, announcing her arrival long before she spoke a word. I viewed her curiously but had no occasion to speak with her. We had no mutual friends, no classes together, never rode the bus with each other and had not gone to the same elementary school so she was a stranger to me. Nonetheless, our paths crossed when a male classmate came up to my locker and stuck a petition in my face.

"We need you to sign this," he said, handing me the clipboard he was carrying.

"What is it?" I asked.

"We're starting a We Hate Leslie Barnett club," he said, without a hint of remorse in his voice.

"Get out of here," I said, my voice going cold.

Having been the target of an identical effort in fifth grade, I immediately empathized deeply with Leslie and left my locker in stunned amazement that kids still did this sort of thing to each other at 13. I felt distraught and sick as all the emotions I'd experienced as a 10-year old came rushing back to me. I remembered what it was like to be singled out for inhumane treatment and how hurtful it was to me.

What I didn't do, however, was anything helpful to Leslie. Other than refusing to sign the petition and hoping the movement would peter out, I didn't confront the idiots who founded the club or report them to the teachers or the principal or anything else. At the time, it never occurred to me that I had the power or the responsibility to do more. If I'd been thinking and had courage, I would have taken action and reached out to Leslie to let her know I stood with her and not them. For some reason, despite being reminded of this cruel effort every time a rogue poster appeared on the wall with the initials W.H.L.B, I didn't do any of that, failing my classmate and failing myself.

Toward the end of the year, my sister entered the high school talent show as a singer. The night of her performance, I was there with my parents in the front of the auditorium, all of us excited to see Pam do what she did best. The song she chose, *Send in the Clowns*, is admittedly maudlin but when a 15-year old girl stands up and sings beautifully and earnestly, it is affecting and within seconds of starting she had everyone enraptured; everyone except some joker from her class who midway through the song decided to throw an egg at her from the back row.

The egg hit its intended target, smashing into Pam's leg and leaving a dripping residue of broken shell and yolk. Most would have run from the stage in embarrassment and upset but not my sister. After the briefest of pauses and a perceptible catch in her throat and moistening of her eyes, she stayed put and finished the song, demonstrating a poise and resolve everyone marveled at with good reason.

As soon as she was done, I raced backstage and found her in tears by a water fountain. I told her how sorry I was and offered a hug which she accepted without hesitation. I felt undeserving of her open arms given my cruel behavior but somehow she knew I was apologizing for all of it and she chose to forgive me. In that moment, realizing how much she meant to me, I made peace with Pam and began rebuilding our relationship.

By June, the Leslie Barnett hate club faded into obscurity, I salvaged a C in band and left eighth grade knowing only two things. I would never listen to Will Simmons again and, though I wasn't the person I wanted to be yet, I was on my way.

6
COMPETITION

The summer after eighth grade, my parents sent me to tennis camp at Hotchkiss, a fancy prep school in Connecticut. I'm not sure why since there were lots of local options. Perhaps they hoped some time among the civilized set would improve my prospects and put me on the path to the Presidency or an ambassadorship. Little did they know the peril they were placing me in as they escorted me to my assigned dorm room and said goodbye for two weeks.

"I'm not sure I fit in here, Dad," I said, eyeballing the cot laid out for me and its woefully thin mattress.

"Nonsense. You're gonna love it," my father enthused, a sure sign it was too late to get out of this catastrophe.

"But the other kids have been here all summer and I'm coming in for the last part," I protested.

"It'll all work out. Now your mother and I need to go," he said, reminding me their first scheduled wine tasting in the Berkshires was only hours away.

My parting words: "I'll never make friends," were a bit dramatic, but they proved prophetic.

After unpacking my things, I headed down to the tennis center, a dilapidated clubhouse surrounded by dozens of courts, for a skills assessment. Following a flurry of introductions, I walked on to the green clay surface and the tennis professionals, none of whom were likely certified to teach tennis, began feeding me balls. Forehands, backhands, volleys, serves and overheads were tested while a shirtless guy with a clipboard took notes.

Ten minutes into the exercise, with a shiny, sweaty face, I notched my first victory. Fritz, the shirtless guy, announced I would be in the top group and would practice with the best campers. I had been playing a lot and was pleased with his assessment.

"This guy might be a match for Heysoose," said Fritz.

"I'm not sure about that," said Barry, another staff pro.

"Who's Heysoose?" I asked.

"You don't know Jesus Loco?" Barry asked as if he was surprised.

"No. I just got here, remember?" I said respectfully.

"Well, everybody knows him. He's a Mexican kid up here from Guadalajara for the summer. His name means Crazy Jesus but everybody calls him Heysoose. He's the best player in the camp," Barry explained.

"You might get to play him in the tournament next week," Fritz said.

"There's a tournament?" I asked.

"Yes. You got here just in time," Fritz said.

Great, I thought, as I returned to my dorm to unpack. *I've been here one hour and I'm on a collision course with Crazy Jesus.*

That evening in the dining hall, I was a model of anonymity, quietly eating my Salisbury steak, green beans and small dish of vanilla ice cream at a long table with twenty strangers. Nobody said a word to me and I didn't mind. At least that's what I told myself as I bussed my tray and followed the crowd to the campus recreation center; where a couple of sad-looking ping pong and pool tables were hopelessly occupied and I sat along the wall, too anxious to start a conversation with anyone.

If it hadn't been for the music coming from the jukebox in the corner, with its beckoning neon lights, I might have given up altogether and retreated to my dorm room. But the machine kept serving up songs, one after another, with the kind of mournful, dreamy atmospherics popular in the late 1970s and perfectly designed to feed the love-starved infatuations of 13-year old boys like me. If England Dan didn't get you, John Ford Coley would. The music mattered and right on cue, with Fleetwood Mac's *Dreams* filling the rec center and entrancing me, someone intriguing interrupted my reverie.

"You're new, aren't you?" a voice said.

I looked up and saw a goddess with golden hair and a mood ring standing in front of me.

"Uh, yes," I choked out.

"I'm Beth, one of the counselors. You looked kind of lonely over here."

My God, this girl can read minds. Must be the mood ring.

"It's tough being the new kid," she continued.

I couldn't believe my luck. With Alan O'Day's *Undercover Angel* playing in the background, I scrambled to come up with a question.

"Where are you from?" I said, expecting her to say a distant planet given her rapturous hold on me.

"Bethesda, Maryland."

I had never heard of Bethesda, Maryland but it didn't matter. I was smitten and happily in love with Beth from Bethesda. This was the greatest camp ever.

Everything was going perfectly - better than perfectly as our conversation flowed like a freshly-Drano'd sink. She liked *Happy Days*. I liked *Happy Days*. She liked Mr. Pibb. I liked Mr. Pibb. What were the odds? This was one of those romantic comedies where the couple meets cute and after a series of mishaps and misunderstandings comes to realize they can't live without each other. In our case, however, we were going to skip the mishaps and proceed directly to happily ever after. At least that's what I was thinking when our first mishap arrived.

"Have you met Heysoose?" Beth asked me out of the blue, her gaze now directed over my shoulder at someone behind me.

Before I could answer, I turned around to see Heysoose's smiling brown face offset by bright white teeth. He was much bigger than me with muscular arms, sweeping shoulder-length black hair and the beginnings of a mustache on his upper lip. To put it in terms of bread, he was a thick, perfectly-cut piece of pumpernickel and I was a thin, wobbly slice of Wonder white with thumb prints. More troubling, the gleam in his eyes told me instantly Crazy Jesus liked Beth from Bethesda the same way I did.

"Hola," Heysoose said to me, extending his hand.

"Hello," I countered, standing up and robotically extending my hand to meet his as the chorus from Dave Mason's *We Just Disagree* echoed overhead.

"Everybody loves Heysoose," Beth said. "Isn't he cute?"

Having met my competition for Beth's affection, I nodded and suddenly felt insecure. Heysoose reminded me of every foreign exchange student I'd seen at my school. They all smiled a lot, spoke little and were loved much for no reason other than their good looks and benign presence. How could I compete with that?

"Are you looking forward to the camp tournament?" Beth asked Heysoose.

"Si," he replied.

"Everybody says you're going to win it," Beth gushed, reaching out and touching him on the arm.

"Si," Heysoose said, purring like a cat getting his fur rubbed.

Horrified by their chemistry, I watched helplessly as Heysoose charmed Beth with a handful of words and a 5th Avenue Bar he casually offered and she gladly accepted. Clearly, this guy had big league moves when it came to the ladies and as I stood there with empty hands, wishing I'd brought a Baby Ruth or a Charleston Chew, I felt outmatched and defeated. From then on, every evening in the rec center, as my crush deepened and 10cc crooned about the *Things You Do For Love* in a seemingly endless loop, I kept coming in second to Heysoose.

Under the gaze of Fritz and the rest of the shirtless pro staff, the same was true on the tennis court. As part of his practice group, I learned firsthand Heysoose had heavy topspin groundstrokes that landed deep in the court and bounced high above my shoulders, making it tough to win points. His shots were suffocating and

High School Dance

each one was punctuated by a grunt so loud I thought he was dying. I looked for weakness but found none and concluded everything I'd been told was true. Not only was Heysoose the best player in the camp, he was also the nicest and the most popular. Campers loved him. Counselors loved him. And, worse yet, I feared the woman I'd set my heart on loved him, too. Still, I couldn't give up and when the tournament arrived the next week, I was inserted as the number two seed, right behind Crazy Jesus, setting up our inevitable match of destiny in the finals. It would be winner take all - the title, the trophy and Beth from Bethesda.

The week of the tournament was the hottest of the whole summer. Temperatures tipped 90 degrees and the humidity made it feel like 100. With a draw of 128 players, the tournament required its winner to prevail in seven matches over seven days. Playing on green clay, a surface that slows the ball down, meant every clash would be physically draining no matter the opponent.

In the first round I drew Peanuts Connelly who was only three feet six inches tall but had a vicious slice backhand. Unfortunately, five games into the first set, Peanuts twisted his ankle and had to be carried off the court while yelling for his mother. My second round foe, Karl "Handy Man" Henderson, was known for playing James Taylor over and over on the jukebox in the rec center. He was also known for being a really crappy player making it easy to get by him. The third round brought a guy everyone referred to as Mad Dog. I quickly learned why as he threw his racket into the fence and yelled out sh@*t! every time he lost a point. After several warnings from the tournament director to calm down, Mad Dog threw his racket over the fence, hit another camper and was promptly defaulted. My fourth round and quarter-final opposition both succumbed to heat stroke and somehow, six grueling days into the event, I was still alive and only one match away from the finals.

Standing in my way was a kid called Visor, a nickname he'd been given due to his enormous headgear. Visor was so skinny and his tennis visor stuck out so far, he looked like a gigantic letter F. Visor was known as a backboard, the kind of player who never misses, but he had an endurance problem. In addition to asthma, he had a sodium deficiency requiring him to gobble salt tablets like Chiclets. If I could keep Visor on the court for at least two hours, I figured I could sink him.

We started at 10:00 a.m. and by Noon; we were tied at one set a piece. To my dismay, Visor proved resilient, relentlessly launching his trademark moon balls, one after another, as rallies frequently reached 30 shots or more. After three hours of play, with the score tied 4-4 in the third set, Visor was popping salt pills and clinging to his inhaler at every changeover, but he wouldn't quit. Under the glaring sun, I felt myself starting to wilt and wondering whether I could outlast him. Until then, my positive thoughts of Beth and reaching the finals had kept me going but now negative thoughts began to creep in like unwanted weeds in a garden. I began to doubt myself. If I didn't win, I wouldn't get the chance to face Heysoose and win Beth over but what difference did it make? I had no chance against Heysoose and Beth liked him better anyway. Why keep going?

In a funk, I lost the next game and fell behind 5-4, leaving Visor only one game away from beating me. At the changeover, I tried to regroup, recounting in my mind all the conversations I'd had with Beth and searching frantically for a reason to hope. All seemed lost but as Visor began coughing and choking on a large handful of GORP he'd eaten too quickly it suddenly came to me. One night in the rec center, with another female counselor by her side, Beth pointed at me and said, "I think he's going to be handsome when he grows up, don't you?" Now I could have interpreted it as intended, namely I was too young for her but had potential or I could have interpreted it as her saying I was a stud and she wanted to bear my children. I chose the latter and convinced myself she liked me the same way I liked her in and nobody but Beth could tell me otherwise. After that, Visor didn't stand a chance and the next thing I knew I was standing at the net victorious and poised to play Heysoose.

The next day, the grandstand abutting court one was full of campers and counselors, over 100 strong, ready to watch the finals. I got nervous when I saw Beth in the crowd and more nervous when I noticed dozens of small Mexican flags on sticks being held by nearly everyone in attendance. Where they found these flags was a mystery but the crowd favorite was not. From the top to the bottom row, they had all come to see Crazy Jesus devour me like a freshly-ripped packet of Pop Rocks.

Heysoose looked like a Mexican Bjorn Borg with his checked Fila attire and long, black hair held back by a headband. The smile I was accustomed to seeing him flash Beth was gone and when I tried to make eye contact, he conspicuously avoided doing the same. Battle-hardened by my prior six matches; I picked at the strings of my aluminum Head Edge and readied myself for the physical and mental struggle about to commence. I refused to be intimidated.

As soon as we started, I felt the power of Heysoose's popularity as the crowd cheered every time he won a point and stayed silent when I did. Up high in the last row of the stands, where the rowdiest fans had gathered, several campers beat bongo drums while a sea of small Mexican flags waved around them urging Heysoose onward. The atmosphere was akin to a Davis Cup match in Acapulco and before I knew it, I was down 3-0. Distracted by the mob and overwhelmed by Heysoose's topspin, I struggled to get my bearings. I searched for Beth in the crowd but found no assurance in her eyes.

Something had to change if I was to have any chance of winning. Going toe to toe with him from the baseline would be futile as he was taller, stronger and more consistent. After losing the first set 6-1 and going down 2-0 in the next, I noticed the harder I hit the ball the harder it came back. Like all enemies, Heysoose loved power and used it to inflict pain. Maybe if I slowed things down and started to alter my shots, like a pitcher using a change-up to frustrate a fast-ball hitter, I would meet with more success.

Sure enough, as I started to slice the ball and take pace off of it, Heysoose began to make mistakes. My new strategy led to the further discovery that Crazy Jesus hated coming to net. He was a creature of the baseline and felt uncomfortable anywhere else. So when I repeatedly dinked the ball short over the net, forcing him to run in, and then lobbed my next shot over his head, he got frustrated. Over and over I employed this technique and miraculously won the second set 7-5, leaving Heysoose and his supporters thoroughly flummoxed.

With the match now even, Heysoose's veneer of cool began to show cracks. It started with muttering under his breath and escalated to him swearing in his native tongue. With eighth grade Spanish under my belt, I knew he was calling me a big, fat, hairy something but I wasn't sure what. Sensing their boy was in trouble, the worried throng doubled down on its support. The bongos beat louder, the flags waved incessantly and a rhythmic chant of "Hey! Soose! Hey! Soose! Hey! Soose!" rang out in the hot, wet, Connecticut wilderness.

The third set was a fist fight with rackets between two soaked sponges. By now, my sweat drops had sweat drops and I felt like someone had shoved a bag of cotton balls into my lungs. Heysoose made adjustments to his strategy and started hitting his own short balls for me to chase. Back and forth we went, shot after shot, betting the other guy would fade first or preferably have a massive stroke. My sweat-soaked shirt clung heavily to my chest like a lead vest at a dental appointment and my legs started to cramp but adrenaline and a banana pushed me past the pain. I was learning how to compete and it was either exhilarating or way too much trouble. I hadn't made up my mind.

At six games all, the referee instructed us to play a nine-point sudden death tiebreaker. As we prepared to start, the chant for my adversary went up again.

"Hey! Soose! Hey! Soose! Hey! Soose!"

I looked up to the stands to see if Beth was part of this vocal pack but her face was obscured.

"Hey! Soose! Hey! Soose! Hey! Soose!"

With the bongos beating and the flags waving, I tried to concentrate on Heysoose. Both of us were spent, but we played on until we reached four all in the tiebreaker and were down to one final point to settle everything. I had never wanted to win anything so much.

Heysoose served the last point, hitting the ball directly at me and jamming me. Luckily, I managed to get my body out of the way and get a good look at it. My backhand return floated before landing just inside the baseline. Heysoose stepped in and fearlessly smashed a forehand down the line forcing me to run and stab at the ball. My return, a short lob, barely made it over the net and sat up high as my momentum took me beyond the court's boundaries. Moving forward, Heysoose was well-positioned to put me away. All he had to do was punch the ball over the net at a reasonably short angle and there would be no chance for me to reach it. Instead, he hesitated in making his shot selection and then tried to compensate by hitting the ball too hard. Flying off his racket, the ball hit the top of the net and lingered there, suspended seemingly forever, as the crowd gasped and I watched helplessly. Finally, it fell back on Heysoose's side. It was over. I had won.

Everyone was stunned into silence, but the brief momentary quiet was immediately pierced by the sound of someone standing up and exuberantly shouting "Yes!" from the grandstand. She was the only one who said a word and her name was Beth. Beth from Bethesda.

7
HEARTBREAK

I fell in love with Casey instantly and hard. I was 15 and standing under a covered picnic area at a local park when I saw her. The occasion was a spontaneous gathering of teenagers in the day when word of mouth was the only social media available and the restless energy of kids about to start a new school year compelled them to seek the company of their peers.

From the start, Casey captured me in a way that left me more vulnerable than I realized. New to the area, she was beautiful but remarkably approachable, having brought a lack of pretension and a love of Springsteen with her from New Jersey, her prior home. I spent the night focused on her bright blue eyes as if doing so intently enough would stop her from leaving my side and even kicked my best friend in the leg when he tried to join our conversation. I didn't want anything to interrupt what was happening. It was pure and perfect and when I leaned in and kissed her before saying goodbye, we arrived at the place every glance had promised to lead.

We weren't officially a couple when school started so I wondered endlessly about our status and looked for her every time I entered the halls, hoping to make eye contact. Casey was a year older and in all different classes so finding her was a challenge, but when I did she let me know she liked me in small, silent ways with her smile and touch and in more obvious ways with her hearty laugh and gentle teasing. Before long, I marshalled my courage and asked her to a movie, *Fast Times at Ridgemont High*, and from then on, like Rat and Stacy, it was Casey and me everywhere.

Other than playing Space Invaders, holding hands with her as we walked around campus gave me greater pleasure than I'd ever experienced. I actually felt pride having her on my arm and imagined every eye on me an envious one. Was our romance any different than the other millions of romances that spring up in high school every year? Of course not, but I thought we were making history. Some people marry their high school sweetheart so why not me. I was ready to sign on and for a fleeting, magical time everything was right. I was the guy in *Jessie's Girl* - funny and cool with the lines - and now Casey was mine. From dance floors to dinners to basement bean bag chairs, we were always together and before long I stopped acting cool and let Casey know how strongly I felt about her. This was a critical error in judgment.

The French say in every relationship there is one who kisses and one who offers the cheek. In our relationship, I was the former and soon learned our survival hinged entirely on Casey's willingness to maintain the status quo. Once she discovered I cared for her more than she cared for me, doubt entered her mind. If he likes *me* this much, there must be something wrong with him. Her emotional withdrawal came first with vague suggestions we might not be right for each other or we might need time apart. But when I protested, it wasn't long before her physical withdrawal arrived. My fumbling for her late at night on her parents' couch, something previously welcomed and encouraged, was now redirected. I was far too inexperienced and far too in love to accept what she was trying to tell me. So I hung on, certain my steadfastness would change her mind and cause her to once again offer her cheek. I was young and stupid and as big a fool as there's ever been, the guy you hear about in the song, and things were about to get worse.

No doubt feeling trapped, Casey tried something else. Calling me up on a Sunday night after a weekend when I'd been out of town with my parents, she tearfully confessed she had made out with someone else at a party the day before - a guy I knew from her class. Surely she hoped I would break things off, but I was too deluded to take the not so subtle hint I needed to move on. Instead, I forgave her and walked through school every day wanting to kill the culprit who'd kissed her and subjecting myself to the humiliation that comes when everyone knows your secret. Things got more and more awkward and painful until one night at her house she came out with it and told me it was over in a way I couldn't dodge. My father picked me up and when I got into his car, I broke into tears and cried like a kid whose bike has been run over by an eighteen-wheeler. I had been rejected by the person I cared about most.

To be sure, having my heart crushed purple did have an upside if you can call it that. Suddenly every maudlin song on the radio about lost love spoke to me and as I dived deeper and deeper into my pool of self-pity, one song above all others gave me strange comfort. *Every Breath You Take* by the Police was released in

May of my sophomore year a month or so after Casey broke up with me and I thanked God for it whenever it came on. Far from being a cheesy or sappy ballad, its cadence and Sting's delivery perfectly captured the yearning and pain I was feeling and spoke to Casey for me at a time when I could no longer speak to her myself. I prayed she was listening and dreamed the song would direct her back to me.

With my torch lit, I kept my distance while continuously looking for a way back into her good graces. And when the school held its carnation sale in early June to raise money for school events, I thought I found it. Sending flowers to Casey anonymously, I signed the accompanying card with the initials EBYT for my favorite song. I didn't know what would come next but I desperately wanted to make a romantic gesture and re-introduce myself as a secret admirer to inject new life into our love story. The reaction was not what I wanted. Soon cornered by her friends at my locker, I was grilled as they demanded to know if I had been the one to send the flowers, something I vigorously denied for self-preservation purposes. One of the girls was cruel enough to inform me Casey hoped they weren't from me. I was devastated but kept my poker face throughout and told no one about what I'd done. As far as I was concerned, this secret would die with me.

The school year ended and *Every Breath You Take* took over the airwaves for the summer. Number one for two months, it invaded your head, your television, your radio and your heart, especially for those of us who were hurting. I listened to it over and over and over again as I thought of Casey every day but didn't see her once. Feeling the way I did, I found it incomprehensible she was glad to be rid of me and hardly thinking of me at all. Like I said, I was seriously delusional.

When school started in the fall, seeing Casey made me sad though I hid it well. Whenever we crossed paths, I would glance over and give her a tight smile but never speak. A September dance was scheduled and I wondered if Casey would attend. A big part of me couldn't let go and believed there was still a chance for us. I wanted her to dance with me. I wanted her to hold me. I wanted her to tell me she'd been wrong. I wanted her back. I wanted so much.

When the dance came, it was held in the school commons where we usually ate lunch. The wide expanse was decorated in maroon and gold, our team colors, and full of welcome back signs. Everyone was dressed casually with teachers and students milling about along one side or another of the enormous room while a few people danced.

Seeing Casey across the commons with her friends, I went on high alert, confirming her hold on me was as strong as ever. After everything that had gone on, I felt half amazed and half ashamed. But as I stood there wondering whether we'd dance or whether she had a boyfriend or whether she gave a flying fig about me anymore, I had a moment of clarity. Summer hadn't altered anything. Casey hadn't changed her mind or come to this dance looking for me and her body language, even from a distance, told me all I needed to know. I was dust and I had to accept it.

The bitterness of this epiphany made my mouth dry so I turned and walked toward the nearest water fountain. Pushing the button, I watched for a moment as the arc of water splashed down on the drain and splattered in a hundred directions. I lowered my head and as the cool liquid hit my lips, I heard an unmistakable thumping, a one-of-a-kind combination of guitar, bass and drums echoing through the commons. It was *Every Breath You Take*.

Instantly, I was in a trance. I turned to see Casey still standing across the commons and started walking toward her. If I'd ever felt more human, I didn't know when. All my naysaying was null and void and I believed again. It was *Breakfast Club*, *Pretty in Pink* and *St. Elmo's Fire* all at the same time - one impossibly amazing unscripted shot at redemption. I was going to show this girl how I felt about her in front of the whole school. Damn the torpedoes, the consequences and anything else that might come my way. I may have been dust but a powerful wind had blown in and temporarily given me form.

When Casey saw me coming she froze emotionless for a moment until her face dissolved into a surrendering smile. Yes, it was me who'd sent the flowers after all. Surrounded by the same worker bees who insisted she didn't want them, the queen shook her head in astonishment as if to say, "I don't know how you managed to do it, but you have rendered me completely defenseless." Silently, I reached past the gaping mouths of the girls who stood guard and confidently offered my hand to Casey who took it and followed me out to the center of the dance floor.

Once there, I held her closely while we rocked slowly to the hypnotic rhythm of the song. We didn't speak but everything I'd swallowed over the prior six months making me so heartsick left my body. All the hurt and humiliation and pain and suffering took flight and what was left was unconditional love. I buried my head in Casey's shoulder and as the bridge of *Every Breath You Take* reached its crescendo and Sting cried, "I keep calling for you baby, baby please," Casey offered her cheek to me once more and I kissed it for the last time. Bruised but triumphant, I left the dance. A few months later, I fell in love with someone else but I never forgot Casey and I'd be willing to bet she never forgot me.

8
FAME

It was all over the news. If you wanted to be an extra in Robert Redford's new baseball movie, *The Natural*, all you had to do was present yourself in the parking lot of Marketplace Mall the next day and climb aboard a bus full of celebrity-obsessed strangers. Even at 16, I knew offers like this didn't come around every day. What could possibly go wrong?

At the time, Robert Redford was arguably the biggest movie star in the world so talk among my friends immediately turned to slipping the grip of tenth grade and taking the hour-plus bus ride to fame or to be specific, Buffalo, where filming was set to take place.

"We've got to do this," my buddy Woody said, brimming with earnestness. "It's a once in a lifetime opportunity."

Woody was a baseball player who liked to swing for the fences.

"Is Redford going to be there?" asked Billy, the point guard on the basketball team and someone accustomed to running the show.

"Of course he's going to be there. He's the star of the movie," I said.

"I don't believe it. Why would Redford go to Buffalo?" Billy asked.

"I don't' know. They probably gave him a million bucks," I said.

"I'd do it for half that," Woody said, a crafty grin spreading across his face.

"I guarantee Redford's going to be there, Billy," I said as confidently as I could knowing he was our ride to the mall.

"Okay, I'll do it. But no backing out," Billy said.

"No backing out," Woody and I repeated.

"And no telling anybody," Billy added. "This is top secret."

"No telling anybody. Top secret," we echoed.

And so it was decided. We'd leave school after lunch the next day to make it to the mall by 1:00 p.m. This would mean skipping the last two periods of the day but surely our teachers would understand given the circumstances. It wasn't really skipping school we convinced ourselves. It was more like a field trip. Now all we had to do was convince our parents.

"You want to go where?" my father asked when I announced our plan.

"Buffalo. To be an extra in a movie. I'm going to be a star, Dad."

"Good Lord. Are you out of your mind?"

"No. This is my shot at immortality."

"Does immortality involve missing school?"

"A little, but everybody's going."

"Everybody?"

"Well, Billy and Woody. And me, if you say yes."

I don't know why but my parents said yes. The answer defied all logic, common sense and parenting manuals, but I didn't pause to question it. I was too excited. Maybe they remembered what it was like to be young and completely unafraid, but the reason didn't matter.

The next day, I put on one of my father's military jackets I found in the front hall closet. The announcements said all extras should wear drab-colored clothing and nothing was drabbier than olive. The dress code made sense. The movie was mostly set in the depression and from everything I'd seen in old news reels, bright colors had not been invented yet.

At school, I could barely concentrate. All thoughts were consumed by our upcoming adventure as I watched the clock like a pot on the boil. Between bells, I made the nerve-wracking discovery someone had broken our no telling pact. People left and right were coming up to me and commenting on our impending departure.

"Hey. Hear you're ditching to go be in that movie. Excellent!" said someone I barely knew.

"When are you guys leaving for Buffalo?" another voice shouted across the hallway.

"Shshh," I said to all pronouncements, terrified teachers would pick up on them and put a violent halt to our plans.

"Hey, O'Dwyer! When are you skipping out? That's awesome, man!"

"Shshh!"

Somehow, like all high school secrets, ours had been spilled and I instantly knew loose-lipped Woody was to blame. His reputation as an open book was notorious and when I finally caught up with him I confronted him.

"Woody, why are you telling everybody about our plans?"

"I've got bad news," he said.

"Me, too. Because of your blabbermouth, everybody knows we're skipping school."

"I can't go anymore," Woody said.

"What?"

"My parents. They said no. I'm sorry."

"But we agreed no backing out."

"I know. Billy can't go either."

"You're kidding. What do I do now?"

Woody wasn't kidding, leaving me in the precarious position of going by myself of giving up on my Hollywood dream. Part of me lost heart and began rationalizing about other opportunities in the future, but assured by Billy he would still drive me to the mall, I fought off my doubts and decided to go. I knew this opportunity was unlikely to come again and I didn't want to miss it even if the academic repercussions of going, which included all but certain detention and possibly suspension, would fall on me alone.

Dressed in my drab coat, I thanked Billy, climbed out of his car and boarded the large tour bus idling in the parking lot at Marketplace Mall. Sitting down in the only spot available, I found myself snugly situated next to a woman dressed in a brown blouse with a large button affixed to it showing a picture of Robert Redford's smiling face.

"I'm Iris. Nice to meet you," she said.

Returning the greeting, I had no idea Iris, a woman of a certain age with a head full of tightly-wound and graying curls, would talk for the entire bus ride.

"I'm the president of the Robert Redford fan club," she announced. "I've seen every one of his movies at least 25 times each."

"Wow," was all I could muster.

"What's your favorite? Mine's *The Way We Were*," she said, not waiting for my answer. "For the life of me, I cannot understand why he and Barbara Streisand aren't married. It's such a shame. I've written several letters to the editor about it."

Without asking her to, Iris peeled every layer of her onion. As the bus rolled on, she told me about her ex-husband, who was still the love of her life despite gambling away her wedding ring. She told me about her ungrateful daughter who called her once a year and about her star-crossed son who was smart enough to be President of the United States but was still living in her basement because of some lousy breaks along the way.

I heard about the people she hated at work especially Jane who'd had the audacity to ask Iris to wear less perfume due to her allergies thereby landing herself on Iris's enemies list. I heard about the neighbors she despised including her arch rival Vera with whom Iris was in the middle of a seventeen-year cold war over some Christmas decorations and a bush Iris said encroached on her property at least eight inches.

"I don't know you well so I probably shouldn't tell you this," Iris started, prompting me to brace myself for something even more personal than what had already been shared.

"You should know so you don't get the wrong idea," she continued. "See I have this rare condition the doctors can't figure out but it causes me to climax spontaneously from time to time."

"Climax?" I asked, fairly certain I knew what she was talking about but hoping I was wrong.

"The big O. Do you know the big O?"

I nodded.

"It's the damnedest thing. Anyway, I didn't want you to be offended if I seem distracted every so often"

HIGH SCHOOL DANCE

I sat slack-jawed, taking in Iris's latest confession. Perhaps this trip to movie stardom came with a higher price tag than I was willing to pay. But there I was, stuck in my seat with no way to escape and the words *no backing out* ringing in my head and mocking me. If my friends could see me now, they would be laughing at me hard.

Arriving at Buffalo's decrepit War Memorial Stadium, the chosen site for the baseball game scenes in the movie, freezing rain pelted our bus's roof. Of course, this didn't stop organizers with bullhorns from herding us along with a dozen or so other busloads of people into the elements, directing everyone to the concrete bowels of the building. I was now cold, soaking wet and standing next to Iris, who reminded everyone within earshot the snack box of pre-packaged food we'd each been promised was nowhere to be seen.

"Where's the snack box?" Iris hollered at anyone she saw with a bullhorn. "We were promised a snack box and I'm hungry as a pregnant woman."

I was hungry, too, but my hunger pangs were playing second fiddle to the discomfort caused by my waterlogged attire. Military jackets from the 1960s were devoid of any features to guard against inclement conditions and the coat was now clinging to me like Saran Wrap.

With no food information forthcoming, we followed the crowd up a series of ramps until we were in the stands overlooking the field. Our seats were covered by an enormous overhang but the whipping win brought in the rain where it continued to hit us in the face. Sitting among us were dozens of plywood seat holders cut out in the shape of people and painted to look like citizens of the 1930s, several of whom Iris engaged in conversation.

"Can you believe we still haven't gotten our snackboxes?" she asked one female cut-out. "By the way, I love your hat."

At first, the grandeur of the stadium and the artifices of the movie set served as temporary distractions from our woes. Signs in the outfield advertised products from a bygone era, cameras down on the field were covered with tarps and a handful of actors dressed up like ballplayers sat in the dugout boxes smoking and peeking out from time to time. We had made it to Hollywood and somewhere close sat Robert Redford or so we hoped.

The thrill, however, faded quickly and the crowd's patience flagged as we waited and froze. After an hour, a production assistant finally addressed the crowd and explained that as long as it was raining, they couldn't film and because they wanted to get some filming done before handing out food, all of us were at the mercy of Mother Nature. All of us except Iris.

"I'm not waiting anymore," she said to me and the cut-outs.

"What do you mean?" I asked.

"To start dinner."

Digging into her purse, Iris reached for what I hoped was a snack she would graciously share. Instead, she pulled out a silver-plated flask.

"This'll cut the cold," she said, opening it and taking a long swig from its lip before offering it up to me. "Hair of the dog?"

"Uh, no thank you," I demurred as the smell of her liquored breath floated up my nostrils.

Two hours later, with the sun down and the stadium lights on, icy rain continued. By now, Iris had finished her flask and was arguing with a plywood cut out over how many times Elizabeth Taylor had been married.

"I'm telling you it's seven. You totally forgot Eddie Fisher!" she shouted.

The rest of the crowd, including me, was numb from hunger, the weather and the profound disappointment of learning the movie business was mundane and far removed from the mythology of California sunshine and glamour. Just when the stars in our eyes were about to flicker out for good, however, things began to change.

The rain stopped. The tech crew uncovered the cameras and the field populated with people conferring in small circles. Soon, the actors, dressed in the white uniforms of the New York Knights, came out from the dugouts with their old-style leather mitts and began warming up like a real team, tossing baseballs back and forth. The opposing team, the Pittsburgh Pirates, wasn't far behind, emerging in their dark, contrasting colors and doing the same. Best of all, a member of the film crew addressed us and said they were going to try and get some filming in after all.

Like a resuscitated patient, the crowd got off the gurney. This was what we'd come for - the lights, the cameras, the chance to be a permanent part of film history. The only piece missing was Redford and it wasn't long before an alleged sighting sent an unmistakable ripple of pleasure through the stands and, in particular, Iris.

"Oh boy. Oh boy. Oh boy," Iris chattered excitedly. "I see him," she said, shaking as she pointed to one of the ballplayers.

"Are you okay?" I asked.

"Something's coming on," Iris blurted.

"Are you going to be sick?"

"That's gotta be Redford down there," she said, elbowing me and flashing a devilish smile. "Oh boy. Oh boy. I can feel it in my nether regions."

Before we knew it, the cameras were rolling, the Pirates were in position in the field and the Knights were gathered in their dugout getting ready to hit. As each Knight emerged to take his place in the batter's box, the momentary possibility the player might be Robert Redford caused the crowd noise to swell and Iris to squeal until it was clear the player was someone else.

"He's next. I know it," Iris declared repeatedly.

Brightly illuminated by the stadium's klieg lights, our dreams of fame, of Redford and of Hollywood immortality, were within our grasp and nothing could take them away. Nothing except more rain.

After a handful of batters, the skies opened again and put an official end to the evening. Back on the bus, we rode home in defeated silence, uncertain whether we'd end up on the cutting room floor like so many before us. Iris fell asleep on my shoulder and didn't awake until we pulled into the parking lot of Marketplace Mall at 2:00 a.m. We said our goodbyes and agreed to keep in touch, something I knew would never happen. I called my father from a Denny's and he picked me up no questions asked.

I've watched *The Natural* many times, but I've never been able to find myself in it. Still, if you get the chance, rent it and look along the first base line about 40 rows up during its climactic scene. There, if you use your imagination, you'll see me rooting hard in my drab olive coat and Iris, having a big O in her brown blouse, both of us happily on our way to stardom.

9
PROM

I'm not sure who we thought we were. Some combination of James Bond, Lord Byron and Bill Murray I suppose but whatever our influences, my closest friend Chris "Party" Pardi and I were intent on showing our girlfriends and the whole world what a prom ought to look like. We had to break boundaries even if they were boundaries nobody else saw or cared about. So two months before the event, we began a series of strategy sessions in the room above my parents' garage where we could brainstorm in an uninterrupted manner.

Two thoroughbreds on amphetamines, we decided right out of the gate to find a hidden place in the woods to retreat to after the dance. I know it sounds obvious now but believe it or not, back in the early 1980s, most high school kids didn't think about establishing a secret campsite when they planned their prom. Poor saps, they were too focused on renting tuxedos and making dinner reservations. Big mistake.

From the beginning, we knew hiking through muddy fields and forests in formal wear in the pitch black would be part of the experience. Of course, if your plans involve camping, you're going to need supplies. Heaven help the dumb bastard who finds himself in the woods during prom with nothing but a corsage and a polyester three-piece from Tuxedo Junction.

We started with a list of the basics: tents, sleeping bags, Sterno, insect repellent, matches, knives, fireworks, rifles. Admittedly it got a little out of control from there.

"You think we need a raft?" Party asked.

"We're not going to be anywhere near water."

"What if it rains a lot?"

"Umbrellas ought to cover it."

"Probably, but it can't hurt to have an inflatable raft. I better bring it. I'll round up some life preservers, too."

Neither of us had spent a day in Boy Scouts but nobody was going to out prepare us.

"We need sleeping bags for the girls," I said.

"Are you crazy?" Party asked. "If they have their own sleeping bags, they'll have no reason to get into ours."

"Good call," I said.

"What can I say? I'm a romantic at heart."

High school boys our age were almost universally focused on how to inebriate the opposite sex so they'd remove their shirts and we were no different. Our weapon of choice, however, was not what you'd think. We didn't waste a moment plotting how to smuggle beer, wine, liquor or even marijuana to the campsite. Not only was the process of obtaining those substances fraught with complications and potential police involvement, they were also inferior stimulants. What you needed if you really wanted to score was incense and we were blessed to have an expert on the team.

"Girls go wild for it," Party insisted.

"Are you sure?"

"Yes, they have some crazy flavors."

"You don't eat it, do you?"

"No, you burn it. The Chinese have been using this stuff to get laid for years. Why do you think they've got a billion people?"

"Incense?"

"Exactly. I say we go with Dragon's Blood or Musk. What do you think?"

"Isn't musk an English Leather thing?"

"You're right. Better go with Dragon's Blood. They also have Frankincense and Myrrh. That's another possibility."

"That might feel like going to see baby Jesus and I'm not sure that's the mood we want to set."

"Good point. If the girls start thinking about religion, we'll never get their bras off. Let's stick with Dragon's Blood. Plus, it's good for warding off evil spirits."

Of course, what would a prom or the after party be without lots of great music. Taking it to a higher level means performing the music yourself. Most leave it to the band or the deejay to handle but they miss out on a lot. Party and I instinctively knew all this so we made plans to bring our trumpets and began practicing. Never mind we were the two worst trumpet players in the history of mankind, nothing was going to stop us from serenading our dates once we had them deep in the bush.

"What song should we play?" I asked.

We only knew four songs between us.

"How about *Jesus Loves Me?*" Party suggested. "I think that'll impress them."

"Remember, we're steering clear of anything religious."

"God, you're right. They hear that and they'll turn into a couple of Mother Theresas. Total disaster. How about the theme to *Star Wars?*" Party asked.

"You think it's romantic enough?" I asked.

"Not sure. What's the first thing that comes to mind when you think about *Star Wars?*" Party asked.

"Chewbacca," I said.

"Okay, so it's a no on that one."

"I've got it. *You Light Up My Life*," I said.

"That's perfect. We come on all innocent like Debby Boone and then light the incense and pounce," Party said.

Making our vision a reality took a lot of work. After finding the perfect location in the woods near Party's house, we spent hours setting up tents, stocking ammunition, blowing up the life raft and arranging equipment. By the time we were done, our Shangri-La looked like a small military encampment.

The night of prom, a small leak of disagreement concerning transportation sprung up. Party wanted to take the 1963 Austin-Healey he and father were fixing up despite the fact it was a highly unreliable two-seater and we had four people to transport.

"Don't you think it's too small?" I asked, diplomatically making the case for my mother's Pontiac Bonneville Safari Wagon.

"You have a chance to show up to prom in a British sports car with two girls on your lap and you want to take a Safari Wagon?"

When he put it like that, the argument was over.

"Just promise me the wheels will stay on," I said, having recently been on a ride with him where the Healey's front right tire somehow got 50 feet in front of car while we were still in motion.

"I'll double-check the tires. I promise."

Dressed in black tuxes and white Chuck Taylor All-Stars, we squeezed into the ever-ailing roadster and went to pick up the girls. After obligatory photo sessions and nervous attempts to convince the fathers our intentions were good, we took off with our dates, Debbie and Tiffany, both of them piled on top of me in the passenger seat.

The girls were best friends and they both looked beautiful that night. Sweet and innocent sophomores, they had no idea what we had planned for them, something Party and I took great pleasure in concealing. By the end of the evening, we hoped to convince them we were the two coolest, craziest, prom paradigm-breaking guys in school, an effort that began the moment we picked them up and continued at dinner.

Where to eat was an important consideration. We wanted to go down market and take the girls to Nick Tahou's, a legendary eatery famous for its garbage plate and dangerous clientele, but it was too far away. We considered the Conesus Inn where your name went on the wall if you ate The Eisenhower, a piece of meat the size of your average ottoman. However, the thought of the maître d' standing over our dates yelling, "Git 'er done," as they forced ten pounds of meat down their gullets seemed a little too extreme.

In contrast, the Crystal Barn, where diamonds and denim were equally at home, offered an elegant atmosphere albeit one without a wall of fame for gluttony. Consistent with the ethos of the evening, we picked it because we viewed it as an unconventional choice and wanted to avoid the long list of usual suspects from Edward's to the Spring House to Richardson's Canal House at all costs. These were places your parents took you to that screamed establishment, something we weren't ready to join yet.

"She'll start with the Caesar salad followed by the ham with raisin sauce," I said when it was time for Debbie to order.

The one thing Party and I knew about fine dining was that the man always ordered for the woman. If only we had known you were supposed to confer with them first.

"I don't want ham," Debbie said.

"You don't?" I said.

"No."

"Scratch the ham. She'll have the prime rib, very rare," I continued undeterred.

"I don't want prime rib either," she said.

"Okay, no prime rib. Tell you what. She'd like the Cornish game hen with scalloped potatoes," I said, moving down the menu.

"No I wouldn't," Debbie said.

"Do you need more time?" the server asked me.

"That's a good idea," I said, rattled by the lack of cooperation I was receiving.

Party had less luck than I did figuring out what his date wanted and eventually we both gave up and let them order for themselves. It was a brief black mark on the evening we chose to ignore.

The theme of the prom was In the Air Tonight, inspired by Phil Collins' song of the same name, and the decorations matched the song's dark and brooding mood, all blacks and purples and swirling Van Gogh clouds. Young and unwearied, we couldn't have felt more different as we arrived in the parking lot, the four of us crammed into Party's Austin-Healey. To Party and me, the event didn't start until we arrived, a delusion we would never shed.

Supremely self-confident, we dragged Debbie and Tiffany to the dance floor and immediately started contorting ourselves like a couple of spasmodic robots on mushrooms. The girls shuffled their feet back and forth and watched in horror as we demonstrated the most unusual dancing anyone would see that night. The faster the song, the faster we moved, circling around the girls like sharks circling two doomed swimmers.

Naturally, we saved our best moves for the slow dances. The moment *Against All Odds* played, the shark attack stopped and we became as vulnerable as two stray puppies from the pound. If heaven existed, we found it holding these girls closely, the warmth of their bodies and the smell of their skin hypnotizing us and daring us to kiss them. Moving my face closer, checking both ways before I crossed the street, I made contact with Debbie's lips and achieved my American dream. Whether it was me or my Brut cologne allowing me to advance, I didn't care.

After prom, while others headed for hotels and parts unknown, we lit out for the woods like a pack of Huck Finns. Parking on the edge of the forest, we drew quizzical stares from the girls and asked them to trust us as we took their hands and led them into the trees. Trudging through the moonlit mix of branches and roots in our formal clothes felt like the height of romance and arriving at our campsite, the girls' eyes revealed the sense of surprise and wonder we hoped to arouse by bringing them there.

"I'm going to light the incense," Party said to me under his breath.

"Sounds good. Just don't burn the place down," I replied.

"Dragon's Blood do your thing," Party directed as he struck a match.

We built a campfire, played our trumpets, ate, drank, laughed and eventually retired to the tents to make out and fall asleep. Around 3:00 a.m., we took the girls home and said goodbye, satisfied we had smashed the paradigm, exceeded their expectations and met our own. Party took me home and I staggered inside, blissfully unaware there would never be another night quite like it.

10
TRUST

Late August in Rochester, New York is quiet and 1984 was no exception. My parents were headed to Boston to pick up my college-aged sister from a summer job and they needed my mother's diesel-powered Pontiac Bonneville Safari Wagon to haul her things, leaving me, a newly-licensed driver, alone with my father's 1983 silver Mazda RX-7.

A poor man's Maserati, the Mazdarati, as my father dubbed it, was a low-slung, two-seater with an all-black interior, pop-up headlights, crank-it-yourself moon-roof and best of all, an impossibly loud stereo and cassette deck. With its rotary engine, the car's performance fell far short of German imports but represented good bang for your mid-life crisis buck. Difficult to get into and agony to get out of for a man of my dad's six-foot plus size, it was beloved nonetheless the way a life preserver is beloved by a drowning man and symbolized one last chance for my 46-year old father to show the world he was still young.

Whether or not I'd be able to drive the Mazadarati in my dad's absence was the subject of great debate. I begged him over and over, insisting I'd be careful while steering him away from the pesky fact I had never driven a stick shift. They say the sins of the father are visited upon the son but so too are the generosities. From hearing his childhood stories, I knew my father wanted to trust me with the Mazdarati the same way, nearly thirty years before, his father trusted him with his car. So after a bit of hemming and hawing, in a beautiful and foolish gesture of love that said I believe in you, he handed me the keys.

Sixty seconds after the Safari Wagon left the driveway, I called my trusted sidekick, Party, a wild man who loved doing stupid things for no reason at all. On a typical night, Party would slurp a plate of hot sauce, snort a pile of black pepper and eat the biggest dead bug he could find before stripping off his clothes and running naked through the neighborhood. To put it mildly, he had a problem with authority. I didn't, making our relationship akin to a parole officer and felon. Beneath the veneer of rebellion and general insanity, I knew Party was a good guy - think maniac with a heart - but I was also well aware of his knack for pulling me off the straight and narrow. So when I told him my mom and dad were out of town for a week and I had the Mazdarati, I could only blame myself for what happened next.

"Come pick me up," Party said.

Party didn't believe in bathing daily, doing homework or wearing pants, but he loved fast cars. Doing as asked, I sped madly over to Party's house with Prince's *Let's Go Crazy* reverberating from the Mazdarati's speakers at full tilt. Life grants a handful of moments where you feel the full, spine-tingling exhilaration of youth and unfettered freedom and this was one of them. I was a preening peacock fanning my feathers to the world, untrammeled by anything I'd encountered to that point. And if I could have remained that way for years to come, it would have been wonderful.

"I know a short-cut back to your house," Party said as he climbed into the passenger seat.

"A short cut?" I asked.

Since our friendship began in sixth grade, our parents had driven us back and forth to each other's homes several hundred times and never once had any of them *mentioned* let alone taken a shortcut.

"Trust me," Party said. "The sooner we get back to your house, the sooner we can call up some girls."

My Party radar, a usually reliable device, signaled me loudly to ignore him but inexplicably I disregarded the warning. Perhaps it was my father's faith in me or the mere mention of girls but, whatever the reason, I decided to trust Party.

The next thing I knew we were on the road traveling in a strange direction with the windows down, roof open and music up, way up, full of the mindless confidence that comes naturally to high school males. With big, fat grins our faces; we were naval aviators, our ceiling and visibility unlimited.

Arriving at the top of an unpaved road Party directed me toward, I came to a stop and surveyed what was ahead.

"This is it," Party said.

"There's no blacktop," I observed.

"Blacktop is overrated," Party insisted.

"Really? I always find it helpful," I said.

"Let's go. Girls are waiting for us, remember?"

Beneath a thick canopy of trees, I could see the initial outline of a narrow dirt road leading steeply downward - a vaguely beautiful but deserted place I'd never been.

"Is this a one-way or two-way road?" I asked.

"Not sure," Party said as he rifled through a vinyl case containing my prized collection of mix tapes. "What difference does it make?"

"Just seems like a good thing to know," I said.

"Let's go! I've got a radical tune I'm putting in," Party said as he opened up one of the cassette boxes.

I took a deep breath, shifted into first gear and put my foot down on the accelerator. The road's initial steep, straight incline was manageable but my momentary confidence evaporated as I felt the Mazdarati picking up speed quickly - too quickly. Suddenly, before I could slow it down, the road curved sharply, first to the right, then to the left. Unhappily aware I was going too fast, I hit the brakes hard and the car began to slide on the dirt, its back end fishtailing to and fro while I frantically tried to steer it back to center.

Things moved in slow motion. In my periphery, I saw Party's mouth hanging open and a bright white cassette tape in his right hand. But with the car's back end beyond my control, my mind rapidly shifted its attention from the trivial to the terrifying and thoughts of what the car would do next. The answer was a 360 degree spin before leaving the road, diving downward and smashing into a deep, dirt embankment.

When we finally came to a stop with a violent, frightening thud, more than half the car was buried in dirt. The force of impact sent mounds of soil through the moon roof, covering Party and me completely. Brown dust particles, made visible by the fractured sunlight penetrating the surrounding forest, billowed into the car through the air conditioning vents and danced around us as we sat stunned. Everything was silent save for our breathing.

Concerned for my friend, I turned my head toward Party who now looked like a life-sized, chocolate Easter bunny. The only bit of white to be seen was the corner of the cassette tape he was holding at the time we crashed and still clung to tightly.

"Are you all right?" I asked.

"I think so. You?"

I nodded.

"Does this mean no Judas Priest?" Party asked, holding up the white cassette.

Without responding, I pushed my door open, climbed out and assessed the damage. The immensity of the trouble I was in threatened to overwhelm me but I wasn't ready to enter the acceptance phase yet. If there was damage to the car, I couldn't see it since everything was covered.

"I think it's okay, Party. I think it's okay," I repeated aloud, hoping that somehow I would dig beneath the dirt and find no injury to the Mazdarati's metal.

In a frenzy, I started excavating with my hands, burrowing ever closer to the front of the car like a crazed squirrel determined to uncover a buried nut. Within seconds, I discovered undeniable proof things were definitely not okay. The front left end was crushed inward and no amount of wishing it away was going to work.

"It's *not* okay, Party. It's *not* okay! Sh@*t!" I shouted.

By now, Party had extricated himself from the car and was standing next to me.

"You know if we can somehow limp this baby back to your house, there's still enough time to call some girls," he said.

"Do you want to die?" I asked. "Just keep it up."

The next minute, a passing delivery truck saw us and stopped.

"You guys need any help?"

"No, not at all," I said, still stuck in denial. "We're good."

After the truck's departure, we managed to unearth the front end of the Mazdarati and push it back up onto the road. Miraculously, it started and I slowly steered the mangled mass the remaining two miles to my house. It was nearly dinner time now and I faced a dilemma. Should I call my father or not?

"You have to call him," Party said.

"You think?"

"No question. It's the right thing to do. You have to do it."

"Since when did you care about doing the right thing?" I asked.

"I'm only looking out for you as a friend," Party replied.

"But I don't want to ruin their vacation," I said, looking for any reason I could find not to call. "Are you sure I have to call?"

"Positive. Absolutely positive," Party assured me.

Hungry, dazed and numb from the day's events, I found the hotel number my parents had left and decided to get it over with like an animal tearing off a leg caught in a trap.

"Yes, may I please speak to Mr. O'Dwyer, one of your guests?"

"I'll put you through," the desk clerk said.

After six unanswered rings, the desk clerk returned.

"I'm afraid there's no answer. May I take a message?"

"Sure, will you tell him his son called and he needs to call home?"

"Very well. We'll give him the message."

I hung up with a deepening sense of dread. Now, I would be sitting by the telephone waiting on the worst call of my life.

"You never should have called him," Party said.

"What?" I blared. "You said I *had* to call him. You said you were *positive*."

"I know. But I thought about it some more and your vacation point was a good one. This is going to wreck it for him."

"Thanks, Party. Thanks a lot."

Unbeknownst to me, things in Boston weren't going any better. Just as he trusted me with the Mazdarati, my father chose to trust my sister with the Safari Wagon when she asked to take it out for one last night of fun with her summer internship friends. Talk about a rotted decision tree.

By the time the Safari Wagon made it back to the hotel, it looked like it was on the losing end of a brawl with the International Brotherhood of Teamsters. And, unfortunately, it was only *after* he had seen the damage my sister had done, that he decided to return my call. Consequently, I didn't know he was already standing at the tippy top of his pissed off ladder when the phone rang at 11:00 p.m.

"Hello?" I answered, praying it was a wrong number.

"Hey, it's Dad. I got your message to call. Everything all right back there?"

"How are things in Boston?" I re-directed, hoping he'd won the lottery or something.

"Well, your sister banged up the car so it could be better."

"Funny you mention that, Dad. See I had a little problem with the Mazdarati."

What followed next is something I've worked hard to block out of my mind over the years. My father was a professional yeller when he wanted to be and this was one of those times he decided to go pro. To his credit, he did inquire as to whether I'd been hurt, albeit very, very briefly, before his barrage. Although it was too late to change course, it dawned on me as I sat there listening to him scream me back to the Stone Age that I had assured him of my personal well-being much too quickly and with far too much certainty. I should have feigned a neck injury or a broken bone perhaps.

By the time my parents returned home two days later, my father had cooled down a little bit but justifiably reminded me daily of the inconveniences I had caused him with my irresponsibility as he dealt with insurers, repairs and driving my mother to work while we were a one-car family. Unsurprisingly, my driving privileges were revoked and my dreams of taking any girl out on a date in the Mazdarati died. Party, who made sure not to be around when my father got back from Boston, asked me to let him know when it was safe for him to come over again. I told him to check back in 20 years.

Life seemed over to me at the time. Aside from my loss of freedom, I had lost the confidence and trust of my father. It was hard back then but, today, when I drive down the same road, long since paved and part of my regular routine, it reminds me of new opportunities rather than lost ones. Things got better because eventually, months and months after the Mazdarati had been repaired and the hassle of driving me everywhere began to take its toll, my dad chose to trust me again with his car. He chose to believe in me and give me another chance. And that act, consisting of equal parts forgiveness, faith and love, is something I'll remember when my own son turns 17 and asks me a simple question.

"Dad, may I borrow your car?"

11
FRIENDSHIP

In the spring of our senior year of high school, my consigliere, Chris "Party" Pardi, approached me about the possibility of securing a spot on the tennis team, figuring I might hold some sway with the coach as the captain of the team.

"I'd like to play on the tennis team this year," he announced as if he ruled the world.

"Party, you're going to have to try out like everyone else. It's competitive," I warned.

"I know. But you'll put in a good word with Coach Nagle, right?"

"Of course. I'll do what I can," I said.

"You gotta work with me on my game," he insisted.

"Are you serious about this?"

"I'm dead serious. I'm Rocky on this thing," Party said, referencing our favorite film character. "*Eye of the Tiger*. Cut me, Mick. Ain't gonna be no rematch. I pity the fool. The whole deal."

"Okay, Rocky. I'll work with you but no messing around."

True to my word, I met Party at the high school courts the next day after school to assess his skill level. After an hour of chasing his wayward balls, I realized turning him into a tennis player was going to be like turning a french fry into a Ferrari. The will was there but the strokes looked like the desperate flailing of someone in the middle of an epileptic seizure.

"Have you ever had a lesson?" I asked.

"Never. I know it's hard to believe," Party said as he hit another shot over the fence behind me. "I guess I just have natural talent."

"Well, you've got something. That's for sure," I demurred, trying hard not to bruise Party's ego in our first session. "Can I make a recommendation that will help?"

"Of course. Go bigger on the serve?"

"No, that's not it," I said.

"Come to net more?" Party asked.

"No, definitely don't do that."

"Keep my shots in the court?"

"That would help but no," I said.

"Okay, then what's the tip?"

"Socks."

"What do you mean?"

"You need to wear socks," I said, motioning down toward his Chuck Taylor All-Stars he was wearing barefoot.

"I don't like socks."

"Maybe so, but on the tennis court, socks are your friend. This is a sport of stops and starts and changes of direction and you're going to end up with the world's worst blisters if you don't wear socks, got it?"

"But I really don't like socks."

"I don't care. Do you want to make the team or not?"

Party paused to think about it.

"Okay, I'll do it."

"Good. That's today's lesson."

"Roger that. Socks it is. You know this is *so* great. I am learning a ton."

After a week's worth of sessions trying to get Party's game in shape for try-outs and give him a reasonable chance of earning a place on the team, I realized he'd be collecting social security before he was ready. To his credit, he worked as hard as anyone I'd ever seen, throwing his body around the court like Boris Becker on steroids and demonstrating a runner's endurance, but the only thing consistently making its way over the net to me was the foul language he employed every time a shot went awry so I decided to abandon Plan A.

Thinking about my predicament and the challenge of getting my friend selected for the squad, it dawned on me Party's lack of ability as a tennis player didn't matter. He was never going to compete in any of the matches so what difference did it make if he played as well as a raccoon plays racquetball. What I needed to focus on and sell to Coach Nagle were the things Party did well and at the top of that list was rooting. Nobody yelled louder, got rowdier or lived for taunting opponents more than Party. Freshman year he won the school superlative for class motor-mouth and Plan B was to put that mouth to good use.

Try-outs drew a better than usual crowd and Coach Nagle gathered us together to explain the process. Coach was a football coach by training who had started babysitting the tennis team 30 years before to make a few extra dollars despite the fact he knew absolutely nothing about tennis. This hadn't changed as far as I could tell but whatever Coach lacked in tennis knowledge, he made up for with his motivational techniques. He believed in tearing you down and then building you back up provided there was enough time at the end. More than anything, Coach liked to win and wasn't above throwing things if he didn't, which earned him the undying loyalty and respect of his players who'd seen clipboards, bags, hats, rackets, water bottles and curse words all fly under his tutelage.

"Everybody here is going to play eight challenge matches this week. At the end, we'll know who came to play tennis and who came to play tiddlywinks," Coach said.

Coach Nagle would have to whittle 30 kids down to a final roster of 12 and the competition would be fierce. Party came prepared with his game face, wearing eye black to try and intimidate the other players. If that didn't do it, he was hoping his headband, on which he had scrawled 'Die Scum!' in permanent marker, would work. From the outset, his fighting spirit was on display. Unfortunately, so was his backhand.

Over the next four days, Party took on all comers in a series of 8-game pro-set challenge matches. He played fat kids, skinny kids, asthmatics, diabetics and one guy with a glass eye, but the result was always the same. He lost.

"You lost to the kid with the glass eye?" I asked, disappointed I didn't have a single win to advertise to Coach Nagle.

"He's a lot tougher than he looks," Party said.

"He can't see half the court," I said.

"Well, I must have been hitting to the wrong half," Party observed.

"Don't worry about it. I've got a plan."

I knew Coach would be making cuts shortly so I went to see him the next day. After some small talk, I got right to the matter at hand.

"So what did you think about Party?" I asked.

"There's an easy cut. I'm not sure he knew which end of the racket to hold."

"But did you see the fight in him? The guy never gives up. We need that kind of energy on the team this year."

"We do?"

"Absolutely. We need a cheerleader and Party is the kind of guy who's going to scream and shout and get everybody on the team fired up. He could be a difference maker against Brighton or Sutherland," I said, naming our rivals for effect.

"Hmmm. I never thought about that. But what if I need him to play?"

"You won't. We'll have plenty of reserves. He'd be a team spirit guy, a mascot like the Phillie Phanatic or the San Diego Chicken."

"The San Diego Chicken? I don't know. There are a lot of guys who are better players. If I keep him, I've got to cut one of those kids."

"I understand. Just think about it," I said.

Over the next few days, I kept working on Coach Nagle, trying to get the seed I planted to sprout. Had I convinced him? The day before spring break, I got my answer. Party made the team, a result that caused some grumbling around school from understandably upset people who'd been cut after demolishing Party during the try-outs. Suddenly, I was facing hostile questions about undue influence from those who knew Party was my best friend and were starting to put two and two together.

"Listen, Party, I'm glad you made the team, but I really stuck my neck out for you on this one," I said.

"I know and I appreciate it."

"Don't make me look bad," I pleaded.

"I won't. Don't worry. I'm totally dedicated to this thing. With a little more work, I could crack the starting line-up."

"Just remember your socks."

The first two weeks of practice were uneventful and I started thinking it was all going to pan out. Cries of impropriety died down and the regular rhythms of the season took hold. Party was proving to be an asset to the team with his enthusiasm and exhortations pushing everyone to work hard as we drove toward what we hoped would be a league championship. Even Coach Nagle seemed happy, enjoying the presence of his own San Diego Chicken. Regrettably, these proved to be the halcyon days.

It was a Friday I'll never forget. I bumped into Party in the school commons around 8:45 a.m. He was eating a bagel and I was on my way to my locker and then class. We exchanged a few inconsequential words and parted ways. Four hours later, Party's girlfriend, Tiffany, accosted me in the hallway with panic in her eyes and voice.

"They can't find Chris," she said, the only person who still called Party by his first name.

"What do you mean?"

"He's missing."

Tiffany proceeded to tell me the whole story. Party left campus during a morning free period with a group of fellow seniors and walked to one of their homes in a neighborhood that backed to the high school. Once there, he helped raid the liquor cabinet and while the others had been smart enough to ditch for the rest of the day, Party decided to return to school. Arriving in health class on the day they were scheduled to practice CPR on a dummy, Party volunteered to be first and was marched down to the nurses's office when his breath and loopy demeanor gave him away. Aware his father, an IRS agent, had been called and was now on his way to the school, Party made a break for it and ran off when the nurse turned her back. Where he was now was anybody's guess.

Although I could already picture Coach Nagle throwing his clipboard at me, my main concern was my friend. Word of Party's disappearance was spreading like mono but it wasn't until Principal Stoller used the PA to ask anyone with information about his whereabouts to report it immediately that the outbreak turned into an epidemic. Nobody could find him but everybody was talking about Party.

Minutes before class let out for the day, the school's search posse located him lying on a grate behind the bushes next to the main entry and called for an ambulance, which arrived simultaneously with the yellow buses scheduled to take everyone home. As hundreds of dismissed students streamed out of the school to the sound of a siren and the sight of flashing red lights, they anxiously awaited a spectacle to ensue. Sure enough, in a matter of seconds, the sea of people was parted by the EMTs pushing Party on a gurney toward their vehicle. Semi-conscious but seemingly roused by the number of onlookers, Party raised a fist from the supine position and the crowd erupted like they'd just seen Jesus. Loaded into the ambulance, Party was cheered the perverse way the young cheer two people squaring off for a fight, ill-equipped to take what they're witnessing seriously.

Unsurprisingly, however, the serious consequences arrived quickly. After his release from the hospital, Party was suspended from school for a week and kicked off the team indefinitely. Coach Nagle expressed his extreme displeasure and disappointment to Party but also to me. He didn't throw anything, but he made clear this was a big embarrassment to him and the team and he considered me partly responsible. Letting Coach down was new to me and I didn't like it. I knew I was at fault and all thoughts turned to atonement. But how? Nothing good would come from condemning my friend. My only option was to rehabilitate him.

"We've got to get you back on the team," I told Party, visiting him in his exiled state, where he stewed like Napoleon on Elba Island.

"What are you talking about? There's no way Nagle is ever going to let me back on the team."

"How do you know?"

"Would *you* let me back on the team?"

"Probably not, but we've got to try."

"I'm persona au gratin," Party insisted.

"You mean persona non grata."

"Whatever. I'm an outcast."

"Tell you what. Lay low and let me soften up Nagle."

"You'd do that?"

"Of course. It's the only way we can prove to him this whole thing wasn't a mistake. We've got to show him you belong on the team and can make a contribution. Something. Anything."

I approached Coach Nagle in his office two weeks into the ordeal.

"So, Coach, when do you think you'll lift Party's suspension?"

"Never."

"Never? That's an awfully long time. Don't you believe in second chances?"

"Yes, but I make exceptions."

"He feels terrible about what happened and do so I."

"That makes three of us but I'm not reinstating him."

"Didn't you ever make a mistake as a kid?" I asked, hoping to appeal to his softer side by triggering a memory of a youthful indiscretion.

"Yes, and I was punished severely," he said.

"Nobody showed you any mercy?"

"No."

"Oh. Well, it was worth a try."

A month went by and Nagle held firm but something on the team was missing. In spite of what occurred, Party's absence at practice and matches was noticeable and all of us, including Coach, felt it. Except when he was passed out in the bushes, he'd been an ideal teammate who awakened the fighting spirit in each person. Nobody else would get in your face after you missed a forehand and demand you do 50 push-ups or challenge everyone to run an extra five laps when we all felt like quitting. It was unspoken but we needed him and with one match to go in the season, Party got a phone call. It was Coach Nagle.

"You're back on the team."

"Coach, I won't let you down."

"You better not. We're playing Irondequoit this week to clinch the league title and I'm going to need you in the line-up at third doubles."

To win the league title, we had to beat Irondequoit, a point that wasn't lost on Party. Coach wasn't only showing him mercy. He was giving him a shot at glory and redemption.

HIGH SCHOOL DANCE

"What if I lose? What if I cost us the title?" Party asked me.

"You won't."

"Nagle might throw a water cooler at me."

"Irondequoit's the worst team in the league. There's nothing to worry about."

Party practiced that week like the Tasmanian Devil and on the day of the match, as we got on the bus for the trip into enemy territory, he looked as focused as I'd ever seen him. Eric Haase, the team's official DJ, turned up his boom box as loud as it would go and the tribal incantations of Queen's *We Will Rock You* echoed through the air, morphing a group of average kids into a band of brothers.

Pulling on to Irondequoit's school grounds, we surveyed the alien shores. Their tennis courts, blacktop with chain-link fencing for nets and basketball poles not ten feet from the painted baselines, were the worst I'd ever seen and made entering their athletic facility feel like entering a prison yard. We expected to win but didn't expect such harsh conditions. Suddenly, things on the bus got quiet and tense.

"Anybody got a beer?" Party quipped, providing the laugh we all needed and drawing a hard stare from Coach Nagle.

"Just kidding," Party added sheepishly.

The singles matches happened first and by the time they were over, we had an insurmountable four nothing lead. Nevertheless, when the doubles began and Party took the court with his partner, Ashwin "Big A" Varma, everyone on our side knew the stakes. After losing the first set 6-3, Party and Big A came back and won a close second. Party played tennis like Rocky Balboa boxed, headfirst and hell-bent, and as the decisive third set began all other matches were over and both team lined the fences to witness the final action.

"C'mon, Big A!" Party shouted at his partner after every shot, whether good or bad, issuing high fives and butt slaps interchangeably.

Deep into the third they went with the momentum swinging back and forth. The cheers grew louder and the crowd grew bigger as they reached three all, four all, five all and finally six all. The match would be decided by tie-breaker.

"Let's go, Party!" I called out. "Ain't gonna be no rematch."

"That's for sure," he called back, a big smile dripping from his face.

Party and Big A won the tie-breaker and the match that day, but we were all with them on that court and the bus ride back to school was the most joyous any of us had experienced. Party was redeemed, I was relieved and with a championship in hand, Coach Nagle was as happy as I'd ever seen him. We could've condemned Party permanently in anger after he stumbled but we didn't and now forgiveness had borne its sweet fruit. Finally, there was something worth drinking to with a friend.

12
SPRING BREAK

My sister and I take great pleasure referring to our father as The Road Warrior. Wholly unoriginal, it speaks perfectly to his historic willingness to drive great distances for little or no reason. Family vacations typically involved the far reaches of uninhabited Canadian provinces that required four days travel after which we'd immediately have to turn around and come home and, to this day, Dad doesn't think twice about hoofing it 300 miles to an army base to buy prescription medication at a $3.00 discount.

What distinguishes Dad is he isn't just enthusiastic about *his* road trips, he's also gung ho on yours. Few things please him more than to hear about someone embarking on a cross-country tour to see the world's biggest picnic basket or ball of lint. Thus, given Dad's propensities, it was no surprise when he heartily endorsed my plan to drive 24 hours straight to Fort Lauderdale with my best friend Party to spend spring break senior year. Though he had to know we were both 17-years old, immature to a fault and likely to kill ourselves in the process, Dad declared it a capital idea. Mom, on the other hand, was not as enthusiastic, particularly when it became clear we'd be taking her car, a mere ten months after I'd totaled my father's.

"How am I going to get around?" she asked.

"I'll drive you. The boys are cooking up something special," Dad said with visions of Annette Funicello and *Beach Blanket Bingo* filling his head.

"I'm worried about their safety," my mother persisted with visions of car wrecks filling hers.

"Alice, they'll be fine. When I was their age, I was drinking beer at gin mills all over New York City," Dad said.

"And didn't you end up in jail?" she asked.

"That was *one* night and it wasn't my fault. How many times do I have to tell you that?"

With permission to go, Party and I turned our attention to our specialty: mission prep.

"Rule number one. We have to be buff," Party announced. "Nobody wears shirts down there."

"Not even the girls?" I asked.

"I don't think so. I'm telling you the place is wild. I'll ask my dad to get us a weight bench and we'll set up a lifting schedule. By the time we hit that beach, we're going to be ripped."

"What about fake IDs?"

"I've already got it covered, Party said, producing a handful of blank SUNY Brockport college ID cards.

"Where did you get those?" I asked.

"Don't ask," Party said, dropping his head and shaking it in shame.

This was good advice and I took it.

"All we have to do is fill them out, add a passport photo and have your mother laminate them," Party said.

"My mother? You want *my* mother to laminate our fake IDs?"

"Well, she's a teacher so she's got access to a lamination machine, right?"

Lamination, the process of putting a plastic coating over paper, was a common practice at the time.

"Did it ever occur to you that my mother might not be in favor of us *having* fake IDs?" I asked.

"Hey, my mother works for the IRS. I can't have her do it. We might get audited," Party said.

"We don't even have jobs. How could they audit us?"

"You clearly don't know the IRS," Party said.

Ultimately, a compromise was struck. I would provide the trip's transportation, my mother's Pontiac Bonneville Safari Wagon, and Party would sneak into the teacher's lounge at school and laminate the IDs.

By the time our departure date arrived in April, everything was in place. A seedy motel room had been secured, Party and I were buff and our fake IDs, christening us Dennis Free and David Soul respectively, were flawless save for the ridiculous names. Even the Pontiac had been transformed with an Alpine radio/cassette player jerry-rigged to the dashboard and enormous speakers placed in the far back, ready to play a non-stop mix of Springsteen, Springfield and El DeBarge.

We packed everything we figured we'd need: suntan lotion, tennis rackets, maps, water pistols, handcuffs and a Hibachi grill, and pulled out of the school parking lot as soon as our last class ended. Of course, after staying up all night getting ready, we were both exhausted and reliant on a heady mix of adrenaline, youth and Tahitian Treat to get us to Florida.

I agreed to handle the first leg to Washington, DC while Party slept. Heading south through central Pennsylvania's hilly terrain taking in the beautiful vistas and occasional adult video store, I felt like Magellan headed for the southern end of South America and quickly concluded I would spend the rest of my life driving America's highways, stopping only for the occasional burger and bathroom break.

This would have been the perfect time to think about why taking this pilgrimage was so important to Party and me but 17-year olds are incapable of introspection so other than the anticipation of seeing hundreds of girls in bikinis, it didn't occur to me that *Born to Run* and Bruce had convinced us that real life was somewhere out here on the road and what we experienced at home was a faded facsimile we needed to shake off. Subconsciously, we were moved by a nagging misguided notion that we'd find the answers to our questions someplace off in the distance. In other words, it was all about the bikinis.

By the time we hit the Maryland state line my head was nodding left and right. Nervous I might fall asleep, I took an exit followed by a few wrong turns and found myself face to face with some angry looking military police holding large guns and waving me off the road. As they approached the car, I decided to wake Party up.

"Hey, Party, get up. It's your turn to drive,"

Coming to and rising groggily from the back seat, he was surprised to say the least.

"Where the hell are we?" Party asked, spotting the armed men walking toward us.

"Not sure," I said as one of the MPs tapped on the window and I began rolling it down.

"Do you boys have business on this base?" he asked, his automatic weapon a foot from my head.

"Base?" I asked, convinced I was about to be shot.

"Yes, this is Fort Meade, a military base," the soldier said.

"No. we don't have any business here. I just made a couple wrong turns."

"You sure did," he said, humorlessly. "I'm going to need to see some identification."

Taking our IDs, the MP walked away and headed for a nearby security booth, giving us the chance to talk.

"How did you get us on a military base?" Party asked angrily.

"It was an accident," I said. "I'm exhausted."

"Spring break in the stockade. I can see it now," Party said.

"Don't push the panic button yet. Wait... here he comes," I said.

With his uniform, helmet, weapon and sunglasses, the MP intimidated me as I stared up at him from the driver's seat.

"Which one of you is Dennis Free?" he asked.

Party's face went white with fear.

"Uh,... Officer, Sir, I may have given you the wrong ID."

"The wrong ID?" the MP asked.

"Okay, Party. Now you can push the panic button," I said.

It took awhile, but after explaining to the MP we were only trying to get to Fort Lauderdale so we could see a wet t-shirt contest before we died, we found him more than charitable. He stopped pointing his gun at us and even recommended a famous bar to check out called the Candy Store. Minutes later, with Party at the wheel, we resumed our ride toward the promised land.

The closer we got to Florida, the shorter our driving endurance became and by the last few hours, neither of us could steer more than 45 minutes without calling for a relief pitcher.

"Don't fall asleep and kill us," I said to Party as we switched places.

"And miss the Candy Store? Not a chance. I'm fresh as a cucumber," he replied.

On we went, eventually encountering the other 350,000 hormonally-crazed maniacs clogging the freeways to Fort Lauderdale. The energy emanating from the cars surrounding us could have powered a hundred high schools.

"Hey, wake up, there's a guy pressing ham," Party shouted excitedly.

"What?" I asked, stirring just in time to see the drunken passenger of a Plymouth pressing his naked butt cheeks up against the car's window as it passed us.

"This is going to be awesome," Party said, anticipating more antics and itching to take part himself. "Why don't you press ham for these girls?" Party asked as we pulled up next to a station wagon full of females.

"I'm not pressing my ham," I said. "I'm trying to sleep back here."

"C'mon. Everybody's doing it. What are you afraid of?"

"I'm not afraid of anything," I declared as I reconsidered and began unbuttoning my pants. "Okay, here goes nothing," I said, launching my rear end toward the closest window.

Unfortunately, unbeknownst to me, the instant I got it up there, traffic shifted and Party passed the station wagon full of girls.

"Are they looking?" I hollered, delighted to be part of the hijinks.

"Put away the ham!" Party called back.

"I can't see the girls. Are they laughing?" I asked.

"Put away the ham!" Party said more forcefully.

HIGH SCHOOL DANCE

Wondering why he was so insistent, I pulled my back end off the window glass and looked to see what kind of response my ham had received. By the look on the faces of the two police officers in the squad car next to us, it didn't get the reaction I was hoping for and I soon found myself explaining my behavior to another set of officials and hoping to avoid indecent exposure charges.

Escaping with a warning, we finally arrived on North Atlantic Boulevard, the waterfront stretch we had dreamed about, the place where the beach, the bars and the babes were waiting just for us. It was every 17-year old boy's fantasy and we wanted to get started right away. After checking into our stereotypically downtrodden motel just off the main drag, we got into our swimsuits and made our way to the light brown sand.

Every square inch of the beach was covered with scantily-clad beauties and muscle-bound beasts.

"Whoa. These guys are more buff than we are," Party observed, making us both feel self-conscious of our more modest physiques.

"Should we put shirts on?" I asked.

"Nah," Party said with mustered swagger.

The scene was so visually stimulating I never imagined we could fall asleep. But after laying out our blankets and settling in, the lack of sleep caught up with us and, at the height of the midday Florida sun, we conked out. Not smart. Being a couple of pasty yankees from upstate New York, we awoke fully baked, our bodies red as Santa's suit.

"I think we better get inside. I'm feeling a little burnt," I said, unaware how bad the damage was to our skin.

That night we found out. As the relative cool of the evening set in, so too did the chills and the need for repeated sprays of Solarcaine. Third degree burns, however, were not going to stop us from experiencing the life we'd been missing so out into the night we went, two pieces of fried chicken in search of some sweet potatoes.

"Now, remember, you're David Soul and I'm Dennis Free," Party said as we began walking down the strip.

"Got it."

"We've got to live these new identities. What's your back story?"

"What do you mean?"

"Your back story. Who is David Soul? What are his likes and dislikes? Is he married? Does he have kids? Girls are going to ask you."

"Party, I'm still wearing braces so David Soul is a high school kid just like me."

"A 26-year old in high school? Who's going to buy that? You have to be a grown up."

"Look. I'm not ready for all that. Plus, the ID is just to get into the bar. We don't have to become these people you dolt."

"I guess you're right. Still, might be fun. I'm going to make Dennis Free the CEO of a small chain of sporting goods stores."

"Knock yourself out, Dennis."

The bouncer at the Candy Store only took a cursory glance at our IDs and soon we were inside a neon lit den of both professional and aspiring party animals. Having never been in a real bar before, we were wide-eyed and awestruck. Everywhere we looked we encountered bare midriffs, beer bongs and burning doobies or what the staff called a typical day at the office. The music, a never ending rotation of Madonna, Wham, Duran Duran, Billy Ocean, Prince, Wang Chung, Culture Club and Hall and Oates, pulsated loudly, prodding us to lose any inhibi-

HIGH SCHOOL DANCE

tions we had. It was a world of freedom and youth with no rules and no grown-ups and we loved it. Over the next five days, we drank what we wanted, ate what we wanted, stayed up all night, kissed girls we'd never see again, witnessed several wet t-shirt contests and got into one enormous fist fight - with each other.

We were getting ready to go out the last evening when we got into an argument whether Timberlands or Wolverines were better winter boots, a question that could only be settled with violence. In a flash, we were rolling around the floor of our cheap motel room wrestling and punching each other, trying desperately to establish dominance over the other guy with a head lock. The thin excuse to throw down proved if you spend too much time with anyone, you'll eventually want to kill them. And as we crashed from bed to nightstand and back, using every dirty trick we could think of to take the other out of this life, the verbal attacks ensued as well.

"How could anyone be stupid enough to drive on to a military base?" Party asked, hitting me below the board shorts.

"That was an honest mistake," I said defensively. "What I want to know is how anyone could be stupid enough to list themselves as six foot six and black on their fake ID when they're five foot eight and white?"

"I was trying to impress girls," Party said, landing a punch to my solar plexus.

"Let me guess," I said, trying to catch my breath. "That was part of your *back* story, right?"

"At least I *have* a back story."

"Yeah, right. The CEO of a small chain of sporting goods stores? What a joke. You wouldn't know a javelin from a jock strap."

A hair bit stronger than Party, I eventually got him in the head lock position and made him say uncle before both of us flopped on our respective beds, our lips bloodies our egos bruised.

"That was dumb, I said, feeling apologetic immediately. "I'm sorry."

"Me, too," Party panted.

"You mean it?" I asked, unaccustomed to apologies from Party.

"Yeah, I mean it. Of course, I still say Wolverines are better boots," he laughed, sending me into hysterics and immediately mending our rift.

The next day, adding to our comedy of errors, I locked the keys inside the Safari Wagon delaying our departure until the police broke into my mother's car. Boisterous and full of high spirits on the drive to Florida, we were noticeably quieter and contemplative during the return. Sure, we'd come, seen and conquered but what now?

Everyone was listening to *Born in the USA* but we listened to *The River* on the way back to New York. It was an appropriate choice, full of songs celebrating the thrill of being alive and others ruefully acknowledging life's painful transitions and losses. We weren't the sons of factory workers, but we got the message. We'd be leaving home soon and it was going to get rough out there. Florida was a preview of what we'd face when we left our small town, the challenge of complete freedom and how to handle it. Burnt, bloodied and anxious to get back to our childhood bedrooms after a single week in Fort Lauderdale, we realized the adjustment awaiting us after graduation was more daunting than we previously thought.

After dropping Party off at his house, I returned to mine and hugged my mom in the kitchen, a bit more appreciatively than before. My dad was out but he'd left me something on my bed - a group of admission letters from various colleges all of which he'd opened. I picked them up and fingered through the envelopes, unfazed by my father's intrusion. He wanted so much for me and my future, and I could never be mad about that. Instead, I sat down on my bed, silently celebrating the good news and thinking about the adventure awaiting me. I wasn't sure what lay ahead, but I was ready to find out.

HOW TO RAISE A GOOD KID

STARBUCK O'DWYER

HOW TO RAISE A GOOD KID
SAMPLE CHAPTERS

1

THE IMPORTANCE OF ENTHUSIASM

Forward Ho

In the spring of 1976, my father had an idea. In celebration of our country's Bicentennial, he would take our whole family cross country on a summer camping expedition. It was a bold stroke given all of us, including him, hated camping. But he was determined to show us the beauty of our great nation and equally committed to doing so on a budget. The way he saw it: why pay for a safe, comfortable hotel room when you can sleep outside at a state park next to dangerous strangers for free.

Nobody has ever mistaken my father for a consensus builder. A product of the patriarchal 1950's, he believes true leaders refuse to be hindered by the pesky input of others, especially family members. Accordingly, he announced our trip the way he announced all major decisions affecting us; at the dinner table when my mother's defenses were down. He knew she would be too exhausted after teaching all day to object to a family vacation, even one involving bug spray and

Sterno, while serving up steaming mounds of beef stroganoff to her brood.

Having learned from years of experience that my father was an irresistible force when it came to his own ideas, my mother immediately set about assessing the damage.

"Will we go for two weeks, honey?" she asked gingerly; keenly aware of my father's tendency to overdo.

"I'm thinking six," he said.

"Six weeks?" she asked, choking on her stroganoff.

As the owner of his own business, my father could take lengthy vacations.

"Six maybe seven," my father said. "You can't see anything in two weeks."

"Not in a tent, though, right?" my mother asked; the fear in her voice rising.

"No, not a tent," he said.

"Oh, thank God," she said.

"Two tents. One for us and one for the kids."

With skill and luck, my mother could sometimes move my father and his ideas in a better direction. In this case, by repeatedly reminding him of the 13 weeks they spent in a tent as a newly married couple and her inability to have a bowel movement during that entire period, she was able to convince him a recreational vehicle with indoor plumbing was in order. Shortly thereafter, he took me to the RV dealership to explore rental options.

On the lot, we were met by Eddie, a salesman with a plaid jacket and a plastic smile, who immediately steered us to a vehicle best described as a battleship on wheels.

"Seems awful big," my father said. "What kind of gas mileage does it get?"

"About four miles a gallon, but if you want to see the country in style this summer, this is the rig I recommend. Climb aboard El Conquistador, gentleman," Eddie said, opening the door for us.

"Spacious," my father said as we moved into its cabin.

"Oh, yeah, real spacious and loaded, too. You've got your master bedroom, your kitchen, your game room, your hi-fi stereo. This baby's even bullet-proof," Eddie crowed.

"Really?" my father asked.

"That's what my manager says," Eddie replied.

"Do you think we'll get shot at during the trip, Dad?" I asked warily.

"Probably not," he said. "But it's a good feature to have just in case."

Unfortunately, as soon as Eddie shared the rental price, my father abandoned the dream of the RV and asked to see an Airstream trailer; an elongated silver cocoon he could hitch to our station wagon.

"These are nice," my father said, running his hand along the Airstream's sleek surface.

"Sure, no doubt," Eddie said. "You're not gonna have all your features as you would with El Conquistador, but the Airstream will get you from A to B."

"That's the goal," my father said. "What's it rent for?" he asked, after we'd toured the interior.

Eddie's answer was similarly unsatisfactory and we soon moved as a group to the farthest end of the lot to find something that was, "better than a tent, but not as good as an Airstream," as my father put it. This left us in the pop-up camper category.

All the pop-up campers looked the same; like oversized ice cream sandwiches when closed and like Jiffy Pop bags when open. They were unsightly to say the least, but the price was right and Eddie assured my father set up was a breeze.

"Just pop the top when you get to the campsite and, 42 quick steps later, you're ready to bunk down for the night."

And with that, a deal was made. My father loved to drive a hard bargain and he clearly felt good as he hitched our new camper to the car. Driving home, however, I inadvertently soured his self-congratulatory mood.

"Do you think Mom will care there's no bathroom?" I asked.

"Let's not mention that yet," he said. "We'll save some surprises for the road."

The day of the trip arrived and it was impossible not to get caught up in my father's enthusiasm.

"Forward Hohhh!" He yelled as we pulled out of our circular driveway; a guttural call to action he would soon have all of us shouting in unison each time the car left its station. He was a master at making you believe you were having fun whether you were or not.

"Isn't this great?" he asked excitedly, as we rolled through Erie, Pennsylvania. "This is the same route Lewis and Clark traveled."

"No, it's not, Dad," my sister said.

"Well, it's similar," he replied.

He was also skilled at convincing you each sight you saw was significant; a true feat considering there was nothing to see between Western New York and Colorado besides Mount Rushmore. He exuded a brand of American optimism; a belief that something better was just around the next corner. And it was futile to resist.

"Kids, what you see before you are the most historic sand dunes in the country," my father said, as we stood in the middle of Indiana Dunes National Park.

"What's so historic about them?" I asked.

"Aren't they magnificent?" he asked, ignoring my question completely. "Wait'll you see what's ahead."

On the road, despite the lack of a DVD player or hand held devices of any kind, my parents tried to keep my sister and me busy with a series of diversions. There were Mad Libs and crossword puzzles, quizzes on state capitols and presidents, and, of course, sing-alongs. There were also frequent sibling fights that broke out in the backseat as we got on each other's nerves and bounced around like errant pinballs, untethered by seatbelts.

Nevertheless, cruising along the highway and crossing state borders, I felt a true sense of adventure for the first time in my life and it was exhilarating. Every evening, I helped my father set up the camper and start a pit-fire, and ate char-grilled food with my family on tin plates. Drifting off to sleep, I listened nervously to the sound of animals in the woods and accepted my mother's assurances no bears lived in the area. Safely ensconced behind the locked screen door of our temporary home, I was becoming an avid outdoorsman.

Inevitably, however, as the days and hours of car travel dragged on and the sun beat down through the windows, I grew restless and began to question the point of the whole exercise. My father had guaranteed us sights that would leave us in awe and wonder, and I was starting to think he had vastly over-promised. Traveling through Illinois, Iowa and Nebraska, I kept waiting to be bowled over, but was met with mile after mile of brown, flat land.

Then, suddenly, just when I thought I'd been bamboozled, along came the Rocky Mountains, emerging on the horizon like the City of Oz. Moving closer and closer, I was transfixed by their growing immensity. I'd never seen anything like them.

"Wow. Are we going right into the mountains?" I asked, my enthusiasm having returned.

"Straight into the belly of the beast," my father said. "We'll climb to almost 13,000 feet above sea level."

"Cool," I said, my excitement evident.

"Forward, hohhh!" we shouted.

Rocky Mountain National Park did not disappoint. Neither did Yellowstone, Bryce, Zion or the Grand Canyon; each one spectacular in its own way. Over the next two weeks, as we camped in these five places, I became a convert to my father's idea and vision. Seeing these places of natural beauty was important, inspiring and historically significant. He was right all along and whatever complaining I'd been doing about long drives and a hot car immediately stopped. As we left the Grand Canyon, I was ready for more.

"So what's next, Dad? Yosemite? Maybe Redwoods?" I asked, having hijacked the guide book my parents were using. "I've always heard good things about Glacier."

"We're not going to any more national parks," my father said.

"We're not?" I asked. "Where are we going?"

"Vegas," my father said.

"Vegas?" I asked.

When my father pulled our Ford Country Squire station wagon into the fountain-clad driveway of Caesar's Palace and handed his keys to the valet, he looked happier than I'd ever seen him. What I hadn't realized was that the rigors of the outdoors had finally caught up with my parents. My father was sick and tired of assembling the pop-up camper and my mother hadn't had a bowel movement in nearly a month. They were ready for a real shower, a king-sized bed and a hot meal served on something other than industrial-strength aluminum. So just like that, with one hotel reservation, our family's great flirtation with nature was over.

Amazingly, my sister and I adjusted quickly to hotel life and were soon ordering room service like pros, watching *Blazing Saddles* on cable TV and begging to play the nickel slots. Along with my parents, we swam and sunbathed by an enormous pool, and grew accustomed to the good life, however brief.

After our stint at Caesar's, we never stayed in the pop-up camper again. The route home, which took us through New Mexico, Texas, Oklahoma, Arkansas and Tennessee, before leading northward to New York, was spent in state capitols like Albuquerque and Little Rock, where we took in the tourist attractions and slept at Holiday Inns.

Although he'd blown the trip budget with motel charges and driven past a number of national monuments and parks we'd originally planned to visit, my father was philosophical about his choices; reminding all of us we'd saved money by renting a pop-up camper and seen all the truly worthwhile sights. Still, as our leader, he wondered whether he'd done the right thing for his wife and his children and whether or not the trip had met the high expectations he set at the beginning. As we arrived home, he revealed himself by asking the one question that could resolve these things in his mind.

"Good family trip, don't you think?" he asked, parking in our driveway and turning his head to face us; his American optimism wavering for just the briefest of seconds.

For once, the man who never solicited our opinions was doing just that.

"Yeah, Dad. It was," I said. "I loved the sand dunes."

"Good trip, Dad," my sister replied.

"It's been a wonderful trip, honey," my mother said.

"Of course it was," he said, reverting to form. "I told you guys."

After unpacking, my father and I climbed back into our station wagon to return the pop-up camper.

"Do you want to do the honors?" he asked me as he put the car in drive.

"Sure," I said, smiling at him. "Forward hohhh!"

2

THE VALUE OF FATHERS

Pals Forever

Around age six, I began to see kids in Cub Scout uniforms everywhere. Their blue shirts and baseball caps appeared harmless enough but the golden handkerchief tied around their necks horrified me. Wearing a tie was the ultimate expression of conformity and I wanted no part of it. So, naturally, I recoiled when my parents asked if I wanted to join a local troop.

Not long after I said no, however, the chance to be part of a different group arose. Keenly aware of my contrarian spirit, my parents took careful steps to avoid scaring me off the opportunity. They described Indian Guides as a loosely banded faction of anarchists; explaining it was more akin to a street gang than a youth organization. "If you don't like it, we'll quit," my father said, and with that assurance I was sold.

In reality, Indian Guides was a program sponsored by the YMCA with the purpose of promoting close relationships between fathers and sons. Originated in 1926 by Harold Keltner, a St. Louis Y director, it was inspired by the teachings of an Ojibway Indian named Joe Friday who spoke about the important role fathers play helping boys become men in Indian culture through hunting, fishing and tracking as well as spiritual and moral development. Hoping to replicate this dynamic in suburban America, Mr. Keltner turned alchemist; mixing traditional Indian activities and symbols with modern life to create Indian Guides.

Our first meeting, like most that would follow, was held in a neighbor's garage at night in the middle of winter. Homes in our neighborhood were small and none of the mothers were foolish enough to believe anything good could come from allowing ten men and their rambunctious sons, soon-to-be wearing war paint, into her living room. This was wise policy given all gatherings commenced with the noisy beating of a ceremonial drum; an event that usually lasted at least 15 minutes as each kid took his turn.

The next order of business at the first meeting was selecting our Indian names. Creativity must have been frowned upon back then because nobody came up with anything cool like Dances with Wolves or Farts like a Pro. Instead it was all big and little as in Big Bear — Little Bear, Big Hawk — Little Hawk and so on. Unfortunately, by the time my father and I got to choose, everything formidable or ferocious was taken and we ended up as Big Cloud — Little Cloud. Seeing the disappointment on my face, my father said we'd have the last laugh when the time came for a rain dance, but I wasn't buying it.

Without an oath to recite or merit badges to pursue, the fathers seemed largely at a loss regarding what to do with us following the banging of the drum and the selection of names. Hunting and fishing were out given the setting and tracking was difficult unless you were tracking a 1973 Chevy Nova; which by now had been moved out of the garage and was sitting in the driveway. Nobody felt like going outside anyway since it was 45 degrees below zero, a typical temperature in Rochester, New York where we lived.

Mostly we ate and drank; activities everyone could agree upon. Despite being inside a sealed garage, host fathers never hesitated to light up their Weber grills. First of all, it was always freezing and the garages were universally unheated. Second, when the smoke from the charcoal got so bad everyone was choking, the Littles, as the boys were known, would take turns manually opening the garage door to let it out; thereby creating an activity for the group.

We didn't have uniforms but we each made vests, cut from tan cloth with fringe around the perimeter, which we coupled with headbands and feathers to create a look similar to Peter Fonda's in *Easy Rider*. Then we added war paint to our faces; transforming ourselves into the living embodiment of all dressed up with nowhere to go as we sat in the garage eating hot dogs and hamburgers and breathing in fumes from the lighter fluid being doused on the briquettes.

As the weeks went on, arts and crafts began to dominate the agenda. Soon, an organization meant to principally involve the great outdoors was largely devoted to sand painting, Popsicle stick architecture and gluing small rocks to twigs. Admittedly, this was the kind of undemanding and unstructured dynamic I'd been promised, but even I was surprised at what seemed like a complete absence of any substance. We didn't learn how to tie knots, start fires or administer CPR. We didn't help little old ladies cross the street or sell cookies for charity. Indian Guides was turning out to be the true antithesis of Cub Scouts and, even though I loved every minute of it, I felt a bit conflicted. Wasn't there supposed to be a purpose to all this?

When Rochester's snowfall finally cleared (sometime around June 1st), our tribe, dubbed the Tuscaroras by my father, made its one and only foray into the woods with a four-day trip to Camp Cory, a YMCA camp located on Keuka Lake an hour away by car. Once there, we came close to achieving what I imagined to be the Indian Guides ideal as we swam, canoed and tried to learn archery without killing each other in the process. At night, we sat around the campfire, roasted marshmallows and sang the songs one sings on such occasions before retiring to cabins with our dads. It was a perfect trip and, as it turned out, it was my last.

I only spent one year in Indian Guides. We moved away and I never saw any of Bigs or the Littles again. And as time went by, I forgot all about them and the fact I'd ever been a part of the program until I was rooting around in my parents' attic one day as a new father and came across a box of childhood clothing my mother had kept. Inside, beneath tee-shirts and Toughskins my mom couldn't bear to part with, was my Indian Guides vest, still adorned with the patch provided by the YMCA she'd sewn on for me.

Looking at the vest, I felt my memories of the experience coming back to me. The patch was circular with the words "INDIAN" and "GUIDES" spread across the top and bottom of its curvature. In the center was an arrowhead with the acronym "YMCA" embedded on it. And had that been all, I may never have remembered nor fully grasped the importance of what transpired so many years before. But, to my good fortune, when I looked a bit closer there was something more on the patch.

Just above the arrowhead, blended into the background, were the words "Father and Son" and below it "Pals Forever" — the official motto of Indian Guides. I paused and thought more about my days as Little Cloud and what this chapter in my life had been all about. It didn't matter our meetings were held in neighborhood garages. It didn't matter all we did was eat, drink and create the world's worst arts and crafts. It didn't even matter none of us learned to hunt, fish or trap anything other than the mouse that once interrupted a meeting at Jeff Brasser's house. None of that was important.

Indian Guides had one sole purpose: fostering close relationships between fathers and sons that would last a lifetime. The founder may have had loftier hopes in terms of the incorporation of Indian-themed activities and culture into the day-to-day functioning of the organization, but I believe he would have been pleased by the incredible tally of hours spent together by fathers and sons because of him and the resulting impact. Sure, the motto was hokey, but did the program work? As for me, it put into motion a pattern of regularly doing things with my dad that made me believe he liked spending time with me as much as I liked spending time with him. And, years later, when I decided to get married, my father was the person I wanted standing next to me as my best man. Pals forever? Absolutely.

3

LOYALTY

Blankie

Pacifiers held no appeal for me as a kid and my thumb rarely made it anywhere near my mouth. Instead, all my loyalties lay with my blanket, Blankie. I suppose I could have named him something more original like Ed or Charlie or Mudflap, but to me only one name truly fit. Placed in my crib shortly after birth, Blankie was a pale yellow piece of thick cotton that became a very close friend of mine and a big part of my childhood.

Blankie was a good listener and never rambled on with big, dumb stories like other people. He was also very cool, especially on hot summer nights when I used him as a pillow; contentedly laying my head down before drifting off to dreams of glory. Blankie was incredibly sturdy. Unlike some dainty blankets I'd seen, Blankie had the consistency of a day-old bagel and was perfect for chewing on. When one corner became soaked with saliva, I moved on to the next; twisting it up and jamming it into my craw — after which I would happily suck like a boy with a straw in an extra-thick milkshake.

Blankie loved to play and brought impressive utility to any game. He could be an ocean, a tent and a mountain all in the course of a single afternoon. He was also remarkably agreeable, something I truly appreciated having encountered my share of difficult playmates. Whatever I wanted to do was okay with him and no matter how late it got, he was never too tired to start something new. Best of all, he had a wide-open calendar so scheduling things with him was a breeze.

As time went on, Blankie and I remained the best of pals — something I never wanted to change. I saw us a lot like Linus and his blanket. Year after year, they met their challenges together whether it was helping Charlie Brown put on the Christmas pageant or battling doubters of The Great Pumpkin. They were a united team with unquestioning devotion to each other and we were the same way.

Occasionally, someone would question Linus's need for a blanket, but he was always able to shoo them away by demonstrating how useful his blanket could be. When faced with the same question myself, I tried Linus's approach but found little success.

It started when I reached kindergarten and was told blankets weren't allowed in school. I didn't understand this policy (neither did Blankie) but after much protest, I relented and broke the bad news to him. To his credit, he took it well and was always waiting for me when I got home; ready to pick back up wherever we'd left off. I made some new friends at school, but none like Blankie.

Unfortunately, with time, I would learn there were lots of places where Blankie's presence was discouraged; everywhere from church and birthday parties to little league baseball tryouts and swimming lessons. It turned out the world was an inhospitable place for a boy and his blanket and I began to hear the whispers that perhaps I was too old to have one. Still, as the pressure to abandon him mounted, I persisted. I'd take him with me every chance I could, enduring the ridicule and stares that accompanied trips to the grocery store, the public library and occasional weddings and funerals; proudly standing by Blankie whatever the cost.

Eventually, everything came to a head when I was eleven and my father threatened to ship me off to the Army (at least that's how I heard it at first).

"Would you like to see the U.S. Military Academy at West Point?" he asked.

"Are you shipping me off to the Army?" I asked.

"No," he said. "Why would you think that?"

"I'll do better in school," I said. "I swear."

"I'm not shipping you anywhere," my father said.

"Is this about Blankie?"

"No. It's not about Blankie."

"Are you sending me away to school?" I asked.

"No. I just thought you'd like to see West Point's campus and maybe take in a football game."

As a member of the Army reserves, my father had a series of meetings at the academy and had arranged for me to tag along.

"So you promise you won't leave me there?"

"I promise," he said.

After agreeing to go, albeit somewhat reluctantly, I packed my suitcase; carefully folding Blankie and laying him gently between my underwear and socks. He always traveled with me so this was no surprise to him. I figured he'd like to see West Point, too. Plus, he was a huge football fan.

My father wanted this trip to make a big impression on me. He believed I was destined for great things and as we drove toward West Point, he explained to me many of our country's legendary leaders were graduates of the academy. He said there was a tradition of excellence and that men like Douglas MacArthur, George S. Patton, Jr. and Dwight Eisenhower, among many others, spent four years there sharpening their skills and preparing to lead America into war. As I listened to my father, I couldn't help but wonder if any of those guys had blankets.

Arriving late at night, we checked into our hotel and prepared for the next day, which promised to be a big one. Blankie and I were both excited so it took us awhile to fall asleep but we finally did with visions of The Long Gray Line, as West Pointers are collectively known, marching lockstep in our minds. But when morning came and I stood dressed and ready to go with Blankie in my hands, my father gave me a funny look.

"You can't bring Blankie with us," he said.

"Why not?"

"Well, we're meeting my commanding officer for starters. I don't think General Thayer would look kindly on it."

"What's he got against blankets?" I asked.

"I don't know, but it doesn't matter. It's against Army regulations."

"They have regulations about blankets?"

"They have regulations about everything," he said.

I paused before opining.

"That is really stupid," I said.

Without a choice, I left Blankie behind once again and set out for adventure. The West Point campus was everything my father had promised; big stone buildings and statues with a view of the Hudson River you could stare at for days. General Thayer wasn't all bad either and even took us to lunch in an enormous mess hall, where we ate with all 4000 cadets at the same time. Observing the students together, the General told me freshmen (plebes as their called) are not allowed to speak unless spoken to by someone older at the table. I told him things pretty much worked the same way at our house and he seemed to understand. After eating, we toured the sports facilities and even met a few of the coaches. As much as it pained me, I had to admit my father was right. West Point was a pretty spectacular place. I just felt badly Blankie hadn't seen it with me.

The next day we saw Army play football, another great experience, and then began the long drive home. For much of the ride, I pondered a potential future for myself at West Point. Wouldn't that be something? I thought. Imagine me as part of The Long Gray Line. I might even end up like Patton and Eisenhower and all those other dead guys my father kept talking about. Yes, the life ahead of me was filled with infinite possibilities.

And then we got back. Bounding into the house, I told my mother about all I'd seen before going upstairs to unpack. After witnessing the way cadets keep their dormitories and uniforms, I was ready to commit myself to keeping my own barracks and clothing a bit tidier. But when I opened my suitcase, I made a horrifying discovery: Blankie was nowhere to be found.

Panicked, I raced down to the car and scoured every inch of it to locate my friend. When my search proved fruitless, I ran back inside and breathlessly relayed my plight to my mother.

"It has to be at the hotel," she said, instantly making me feel a bit better.

"You think so?" I asked.

"Yes," she said. "Your father will call right away."

Sure enough, within minutes, my father was on the telephone; first with the front desk and then with housekeeping. He explained the situation and was told they would conduct a thorough search and get back to him.

For hours, I kept a vigil by the telephone. With Blankie missing, I felt paralyzed. In agony, I retraced every one of my steps in my mind and struggled to recall where I might have lost my best friend. How could this have happened on my watch? I bet Eisenhower never lost his blanket. Clearly, I wasn't West Point material.

Finally, the hotel called. No luck. They looked everywhere and even inquired with the chambermaid who cleaned our room. Nobody had seen Blankie. He was gone — ripped from my life forever. Upon receiving the news, I cried harder than I'd ever cried before. My parents tried to comfort me but I was inconsolable. I had let my childhood pal down and there was no way to change it. Somewhere out there was a lonely blanket wondering why I'd cut him loose. I was devastated.

And then I got angry. As I contemplated a future without Blankie, it dawned on me foul play must have been involved. After all, blankets, even ones as gifted as mine, didn't just up and walk away.

"Dad, did you get rid of Blankie on purpose?" I asked, my lip quivering.

"No," he replied, looking ashen.

"You did, didn't you? You thought I was too old to have a blanket so you threw him out when I wasn't looking."

"That's not true," he said.

"Was it General Thayer?"

"No. General Thayer didn't touch your blanket."

"Then who did?" I asked, demanding an answer.

"I don't know," my father replied.

To this day, I don't know what happened to Blankie at West Point that weekend. Looking back, I see that losing him was one of life's necessary passages. I have a friend who still carries around her childhood doll and it's kind of creepy; so if my father threw Blankie out, I suppose he did me a favor. What happened to me at West Point was just part of growing up, something I knew I had to do even back then when I was a kid. I just wish it hadn't hurt so much.

23

LOVE AND MARRIAGE

50 Years On

From time to time, when my parents took a trip, they left my sister and me with our grandparents. To get to Grandma and Granddad's place, we never went "over the river and through the woods" as the old song goes. We took the New York State Thruway; exiting somewhere around Schenectady and driving south to a speck of a town called Esperance. Bea and Red (as others called them) retired there after a life near New York City; buying some land and building a pretty, yellow ranch home on a hill with a long view of the valley below. It was a quiet, out-of-the-way spot that felt like Mars to me each time I landed. And though I complained there was nothing to do during these visits, I now see how lucky I was to be bored; a condition that allowed me to slow down and see things I'd never forget.

It's been thirty years, but my memories of their house are vivid. My grandmother had extensive gardens and, come summertime, her sunflowers craned toward our car to greet us as we pulled into the driveway. The yard was perfectly kept thanks to my grandfather, who seemingly spent half his time with a lawnmower and the other half with a rake. When the front door opened, I always smelled something funny: a faintly sweet and comforting scent from cigars, pipes and cigarettes; although admittedly I failed to recognize the source back then. It was just the way Grandma and Granddad smelled. Looking back, I'm sure I inhaled enough second hand smoke to bring a class-action lawsuit against them, but the other things I breathed in while visiting more than made up for any damage to my lungs. To my great benefit, I got to observe, up close and personal, the real life functioning of a lifelong marriage. This was no small thing and the lessons I learned by watching their well-oiled machine of matrimony were many.

For starters, it's absolutely critical to marry someone whose strengths complement your weaknesses. For instance, my grandmother was quite excitable. She could go from zero to DEFCON 1 in an instant if a crisis arose; such as the discovery of low levels of milk, fruit salad or flavored icy pops. My grandfather on the other hand was a calming presence who could diffuse such a situation by reminding my grandmother of the extra icy pops in the basement freezer or by insisting he wasn't in the mood for fruit salad that night. This kept her happy and prevented any number of aneurysms.

Another thing I came to truly understand was the importance of a solid transportation plan in a relationship. My grandmother couldn't drive or, more accurately, *wouldn't* drive after the "incident" in '64 which she steadfastly refused to discuss. My mom said it involved ice, snow and a department store Santa Claus, but the details were sketchy. Fortunately, my grandfather was licensed to operate a motor vehicle in the State of New York and enjoyed firing up his Nash Rambler and ferrying Grandma back and forth from Price Chopper, where she could stock up on frozen corn niblets, more icy pops and enough canned goods to survive a nuclear holocaust.

Couples, I concluded, must stick together in sickness and in health, but particularly in sickness. My grandmother had a lot of illnesses. By her own count, she'd had 23 major operations and she took a special pride in showing her grandchildren the damage surgery and time had wrought. For me, this meant witnessing her mastectomy scar (on several separate occasions), her false teeth, and her psoriasis, among other things, and hearing in-depth tales of Scarlet Fever, arthritis, cataracts and loosened stool. By God's good graces, my grandfather knew the way to the hospital and possessed a special affection for waiting rooms where he could pretend to read magazines like *Redbook* and *Ladies Home Journal*. The fact Grandma was battling three or four diseases at any given time and had a nightstand full of enough prescription medication to make Elvis blush never seemed to faze him. He just kept taking her to the doctor.

At the same time, although devotion and togetherness are wonderful, it's important not to lose yourself in a marriage. This means maintaining your own interests; something my grandparents managed to do quite well. Adhering to the old adage about standing side by side like pillars supporting the same roof, they could go hours without talking to each other; my grandfather listening to Dixieland in the living room while my grandmother sat at the end of her bed watching a nine-inch black and white portable TV, pausing only for meals. My grandfather relished being left alone and, lucky for him, my grandmother respected and honored that wish. Of course, there were exceptions; like if there was a fly to kill in the bedroom or something big like that, in which case she'd holler for my grandfather like she was on fire. But for the most part, she only did that every 10 minutes or so and the rest of the time she left him in total peace.

Money can be an issue in a marriage so you have to agree on a mutually satisfactory fiscal path. My grandfather didn't believe in credit cards and, by coincidence, my grandmother didn't have any; so they were well-matched on this account. Cash and carry was their policy; one that turned my grandmother into a first-rate haggler. To my grandfather's great satisfaction, his wife could acquire her entire winter wardrobe in an afternoon at Two Guys with nothing but a twenty dollar bill and a coupon for kitty litter.

And speaking of wardrobes, it is a mistake to subject your spouse to any kind of extreme makeover; wasting money on things they'll never wear. Instead, you must develop an appreciation for your better half's unique sense of style; a rule my grandparents abided by assiduously. Although my grandmother's clothes were a campaign of shock and awe comprised of brightly-colored, loose-fitting, floral tablecloths with openings for her appendages, I never heard my grandfather heap anything on her but praise. Even copious amounts of costume jewelry in a shade completely unrelated to the rest of her outfit drew nothing but an approving smile. To him, she was beautiful.

Admiration aside, like any twosome, Bea and Red weren't always in perfect harmony. Some people think when two people argue constantly their marriage must be an unhappy one. This is not so. My grandparents loved to bicker about pretty much anything and especially about the weather, what to eat for dinner, President Nixon and the televangelist my grandfather thought was channeling God. The biggest blow-ups, however, stemmed from my grandmother's status as America's most notorious backseat driver. At any given moment, she would hijack a perfectly pleasant drive by screaming, "Watch out, Red!" at 200 decibels. This would occur about 12 times during an average twenty minute trip until we finally made it home. For some reason, these outbursts always made my grandfather thirsty; for as soon as we pulled into the driveway, he would mutter, "I need a drink." For the most part, if any conversation in the car or elsewhere got too heated, my grandfather would take the high road by pronouncing my grandmother's position, "completely asinine," and then retreating to the garage to refinish a piece of furniture or build a dinette set; which brings me to another key point.

When tensions boil over in a relationship, it is helpful if each side has a place to escape to for awhile to regain their equilibrium and remember what it is they like about the other person. My grandfather went to the garage, but Grandma's domain was her kitchen, an all-tangerine affair where she was free to smoke Carltons, drink Sanka and ponder the next porcelain figurine to add to her Li'l Stinkers collection. If she'd had cross words with Granddad, she could be found at the circular pine table where we ate most meals rubbing her hands together, worrying aloud about the price of butter and debating whether or not she had enough ribbon candy in the event of a Soviet invasion. Eventually, they'd both cool down and normalcy would resume.

Through it all, what I saw was marriage requires sacrifice and devotion more than anything. Whatever my grandmother's faults or eccentricities, nobody topped her in these two areas. A city kid from Brooklyn, she never shared my grandfather's dream of retiring to the country but she embraced it for him without complaint and set about the task of making their home as warm and welcoming as any. She cooked and cleaned and sewed and, on occasion, when she heard a jazz song emanating from the living room that she liked, such as *Bill Bailey*, she would saunter in and start dancing like a flapper girl with one hand in the air and the other pressed against her stomach; shimmying forward and back and singing with a huge smile on her face; telling my grandfather in her own way that she was happy with him and happy with her life. She did loads of laundry and dishes, wrote hundreds of Christmas cards and thank you notes, took thousands of car trips, and ran the household day after day, year after year; always by my grandfather's side.

In the summer of 1981, our entire family gathered at The Old Tavern, a restored inn in Grafton, Vermont, to celebrate my grandparents' 50th wedding anniversary. Having met at college in the 1920's, married in 1931, welcomed daughters in 1936 and 1940 and raised their family, they had done it all and this was to be their crowning moment. On a beautiful July evening, with the sun setting and everyone looking just so, we moved as a group to a converted barn on the inn's property where appetizers and drinks awaited. There was talk and laughter and the frivolity that accompanies large groups of grandchildren. As we ate and drank, the evening progressed like any other at a family reunion until my grandfather asked us to clear the dance floor; a space that doubled as the cocktail area.

He had brought a portable tape recorder which he cued up with music he brought from home. Stepping aside to give them room, our eyes turned to Bea and Red. But at that moment, they only had eyes for each other. Leading my grandmother by the hand, my grandfather wore a handsome summer suit with a tulip in his lapel. She was dressed in a sunny, yellow pantsuit she'd made herself and a corsage; looking lovely and ready to follow her husband anywhere.

The music started and, like Gene Kelly from a bygone era, my grandfather took my grandmother into his arms and led her the way a man is meant to lead a woman; humbly aware and fully certain he is nothing without her. And as they danced, everything fell away; all the years full of joy and sadness, all the good and bad they'd encountered. It all vanished, leaving only the two of them; stripped down to nothing but what they meant to each other. Face to face they gazed intently as age and time ceased to matter and the world stood still. Everyone in the room stood silent and watched; honored to be in their presence and grateful to see firsthand what the fruit of fifty years looked like. It was the purest expression of love I'd ever witnessed and I wanted the song to go on and on.

Unfortunately, I soon learned life doesn't work that way. A year later, the persistent cough we'd all noticed in Vermont turned out to be something more serious. My grandfather had cancer and died just before Thanksgiving in 1982. He was cremated and, instead of a formal funeral, we sat in a circle in the same living room where he played his beloved Dixieland and smoked his cigars, and talked about how much we'd miss him. With one look at my grandmother, I knew she would never get over it. There are some blows in life from which you don't recover. And for that reason, it was the saddest day of my life. She is gone now, too. But when I think of Bea and Red, I picture them on that dance floor; spinning, smiling and deeply in love — forever.

Made in the USA
Charleston, SC
01 April 2016